HILARIOUS
ONE
LINERS

HILARIOUS ONE LINERS

PLUS MANY JOKES A BIT LONGER
AND SOME JOKES A LOT LONGER
AND ALL OF THEM HILARIOUS

Edited by Marcia Kamien

Assistant Editor: Kelcey Otten

Platinum Press, LLC

2015

COPYRIGHT PAGE

Cover by Carol Russo Design

ISBN 978-1-879582-80-4

Printed and bound in the United States of America

First Edition

987654321

CONTENTS

Dedicated to

Marcia Kamien

New York Times bestselling author
– loving wife, mother and
grandmother.

We will miss you.

FIVE-STAR
ONE
LINERS

THOUGHTS ABOUT MARRIAGE

Marriage means commitment.
But then, so does insanity.

By all means, marry. If you get a good wife,
you'll be happy. If you get a bad one, you'll
become a philosopher.   -Socrates

Women inspire us to great things, and
prevent us from achieving them.

When a man steals your wife, there is no
better revenge than to let him keep her.
                              -King David

After marriage, husband and wife become
two sides of a coin; they can't face each
other, yet they still stay together.
                              -Sasha Guitry

The great question, which I have not been
able to answer is... What does a woman
want?   -A. Dumas

You know what I did before I got married?
Anything I wanted to!

Two secrets to keep your marriage alive and well:

1. Whenever you're wrong, admit it.
2. Whenever you're right, shut up.

First guy: My wife's an angel!
Second guy: You're lucky. Mine's still alive!

Some people ask the secret of our long marriage. We take time to go to a restaurant two times a week. A little candlelight, dinner, soft music, and dancing. She goes on Tuesdays, I go on Fridays

There's a way of transferring funds that's even faster than electronic banking. It's called marriage.

I've had bad luck with both my wives. The first one left me and the second one didn't.

The most effective way to remember your wife's birthday is to forget it once.

My wife and I were perfectly happy for twenty years. Then we met. -H.Youngman

A good wife always forgives her husband when she's wrong.   -Rodney Dangerfield

Wife: Do you want dinner? Husband: Sure. What are my options? Wife: Yes or no.

Nothing's more expensive than a girl who's free for the evening.

To vacillate or not to vacillate, that is the question.
Or is it?

In two days, yesterday will be tomorrow.

An elderly man went to his doctor. "I think I'm getting senile," he said. "Sometimes I forget to zip up. "Don't worry," said the doctor. "Senility is when you forget to zip DOWN."

AWESOME QUOTES

Telling someone he looks healthy isn't a compliment; it's a second opinion.
                                    -Fran Lebowitz

If you are young and drink a great deal, it will spoil your health, slow your mind, make you fat...or, in other words, turn you into an adult.

-P.J. O'Rourke

How about those people in Hawaii who live next to an active volcano and then wonder why they have lava in their living rooms?

-George Carlin

Suicide is our way of saying to God, "You can't fire me. I quit."

-Bill Maher

A child can only go so far in life without potty training. It is no coincidence that six out of the last seven presidents were potty trained, not to mention nearly half of the state legislators.   -Dave Barry

Jews and blacks fighting each other. That's got to be the dumbest thing I've ever heard. What are we fighting about--who's got the most people in show business?

-Jon Stewart

The difference between sex and death? You can die alone and no one will make fun of you.

-Woody Allen

I figure that if the children are alive when my husband gets home, I've done my job.

-Roseanne Barr

You can tell a lot about a woman's mood just by looking at her hands. For instance, if she is holding a gun, she's probably angry.

Gone are the days when girls cooked like their mothers. Now they drink like their fathers.

"Drink responsibly" means "don't spill it."

I'm so broke. If somebody tried to rob me right now, they would just be practicing.

I'm not saying let's go kill all the stupid people, no, no. I'm just saying let's remove all the warning labels and let the problem sort itself out.

I changed my car horn to the sound of gun shots. People move out of the way much faster now.

The next time a stranger starts talking to me when I'm alone, I will look at them and whisper quietly: "You can see me?"

"Vegetarian" is an ancient Indian word meaning "bad hunter."

"I think it's just terrible and disgusting how everyone has treated Lance Armstrong, especially after what he achieved, winning seven Tour de France races while on drugs. When I was on drugs, I couldn't even find my bike..." -Willie Nelson

The Secret of Enjoying a Good Wine:
1. Open the bottle and allow it to breathe.
2. If it doesn't look like it's breathing, give it mouth to mouth.

Some days, the best thing about my job is that the chair spins.

I get more cleaning done in the ten minutes before company comes than I do in a week.

Women are like cell phones. They like to be held and talked to. But if you push the wrong button, you're likely to be disconnected.

The boss asks the new employee: "Do you believe in life after death?"
"Why, yes I do," he replied.
"I thought as much," says the boss.
"Yesterday, after you left to go to your brother's funeral, he stopped by to see you."

Condoms don't guarantee safe sex any more. A friend of mine was wearing one when he was shot by the woman's husband.

A guy broke into my apartment last week. He didn't take my TV, just the remote. Now he drives by and changes the channels.

Oh, you hate your job? Why didn't you say so? There's a support group for that. It's called EVERYBODY and they meet at the bar.

"Hi, this is Tom. If you are the phone company, I already sent the check. If you are my parents, please send money. If you are my financial institution, you didn't lend me enough. If you are a female, don't worry, I have plenty of money."

Breathe in. Breathe out. Breathe in. Breathe out. Forget this and attaining enlightenment will be the least of your problems.

The four basic food groups: fresh, fast, frozen, and junk.

How most men propose marriage:
"You're going to have a WHAT?"

Proofread carefully to see if you any words out.

Can you learn to read from a "Learning to Read for Dummies" book?

A fanatic is someone who can't change his mind and won't change the subject.

Holy smoke: a church on fire.

If you are going through Hell, keep going.

Life is just a phase you're going through.
You'll get over it.

I'm on a thirty day diet. So far, I've lost
fifteen days.

You make the beds, you do the dishes—and
six months later you have to start all over
again.   -Joan Rivers (RIP)

I'm as sound as a dollar, but I'll get better.

If money talks, all mine says is, "bye- bye."

I used to be indecisive. Now? I'm not so
sure.

If you leave me, can I come, too?

Every family has one weird relative.
If you don't know who it is, it's probably
you.

You can live to be a hundred if you give up all the things that make you want to live to be a hundred.

-Woody Allen

Ladies, if a man says he will fix it, he will. There is no need to remind him every six months about it.

Politicians are like diapers. They should be changed frequently, and for the same reasons.

-Benjamin Franklin

When I'm sad, I sing. And then I realize that my voice is much worse than my problems.

The doctor gave Mr. Smith six months to live. Smith couldn't pay his bill, so the doctor gave him another six months.

I've been in love with the same woman for 39 years. If my wife finds out, she'll kill me.

A car hits an elderly Jewish man. The paramedic asks, "Are you comfortable?" The man answers: "I make a living."

My wife was in the salon for two hours... and that was only for the estimate.

You don't stop having fun when you get old... You get old when you stop having fun.

HUSBAND: Honey, what's the password for our email?
WIFE: Our anniversary date.
(hours later, husband still at the computer)
HUSBAND: She did that on purpose.

THE MODERN WAY OF THE BUDDHA

Zen is not easy. It takes effort to attain nothingness. And then what do you have?

The Bible says, Love your neighbor as yourself. The Buddha says, There is no self. So maybe we're off the hook?
If there is no self, then whose arthritis is this?

Drink tea and nourish life. With the first sip, joy; with the second sip, satisfaction; with the third, peace; with the fourth, a Danish.

Accept misfortune as a blessing. Do not wish for perfect health or a life without problems. If not for problems, what would we have to talk about?

There is no escaping karma. In a previous life, you never called, you never wrote, you never visited. And whose fault was that?

Be aware of your body. Be aware of your perceptions.
Remember not every physical sensation is a symptom of a terminal illness.

A Jewish mother gives her son a brown shirt and a blue shirt for his birthday. On the next visit he wears the brown one. The mother says, "What's the matter, "Don't you like the blue one?"

Middle-aged woman in dress shop, to saleswoman: "Do you have this in a size for people who actually eat?"

If God dropped acid, would he see people?

Skeleton is taking a stroll down Main Street in the middle of the night, and sees another skeleton carrying a gravestone.
"Hey, what's with the heavy gravestone, buddy?"
"I always like to have ID with me."

Why did Dorothy get lost in Oz?
She had three men giving her directions.

Do you believe in love at first sight or do I have to walk by you again.

Why is 6 afraid of 7?
Because 7, 8, 9.

Manager: What is your greatest weakness?
Applicant: Honesty.
Manager: I don't think honesty is a weakness.
Applicant: I don't care what you think.

If drinking and driving is illegal, why do bars have parking lots?

Your wedding ring is on the wrong finger.
Yes I know, I married the wrong man.

DYSLEXICS, UNTIE!

It's funny when my girlfriend gives me the "silent treatment."
She thinks it's a punishment!

Never buy a car you can't push.

If you lend someone $20 and never see that person again, it was probably worth it.

Drive carefully. It isn't only cars that can be recalled by their maker.

Never put both feet in your mouth at the same time because then you won't have a leg to stand on.

When everything's coming your way, you're in the wrong lane.

I'm writing a book about reverse psychology.
Please don't buy it.

My ex is living proof of how stupid I can be.

I want one of those jobs where people ask, "You mean they pay you for doing this?"

Men have feelings, too. For example, we feel hungry.

I tried exercise but I was allergic to it. My skin flushed, my heart raced, I got sweaty and short of breath. Very dangerous.

I once won an argument with a woman... in this dream I had.

For the rich, there's THERAPY. For the rest of us... CHOCOLATE.

NASA's robot Curiosity landed on Mars. Early pictures show no signs of ESPN, beer, or porn. This makes it very clear that men are NOT from Mars.

On average, any American man will have sex two to three times a week, whereas a Japanese man will have sex only once or twice a year. This is upsetting news to me, as I had no idea I was Japanese.

I hope they never find life on another planet... because sure as hell our government will start sending them money.

I ate four cans of alphabet soup and just took the biggest vowel movement ever.

A mother mouse and her baby were walking along, when all of a sudden, a cat sprang out at them.
The mother mouse shouted: "BARK!" and the cat turned and ran away.
"See?" said Mama mouse. "Now you see why it's important to learn a foreign language!"

I am a nobody. Nobody is perfect.
Therefore, I am perfect.

During a woman's medical exam, the doctor says, "Your heart, lungs, pulse and blood pressure are all fine. Now let me see the part that gets you ladies into all kinds of trouble." The woman begins removing her underwear but is stopped by the doctor. "No! No! Don't remove your clothes! Just stick out your tongue!"

The judge admonished the witness.
"Do you understand that you have sworn to tell the truth?"
"Yes, Your Honor, I do."
"Do you understand what will happen if you are not truthful?"
"Sure," said the witness. "My side will win."

An agricultural student said to a farmer, "Your methods are so old-fashioned, I won't be surprised if this tree will give you less than 20 pounds of apples."
"Me, neither," said the farmer. "It's a pear tree."

I want to die in my sleep, like my grandfather... not screaming in terror like the passengers in his car.

A bartender is just a pharmacist with a limited inventory.

Red meat is not bad for you. Fuzzy green meat is bad for you.

I'm not your type. I'm not inflatable.

Kentucky: 5 million people, 15 last names.

Never play strip poker with a nudist. They have nothing to lose.

THE WONDERFUL WORD PLAY OF YOGI BERRA

We made too many wrong mistakes.

You can observe a lot just by watching.

It's like déjà vu all over again.

A nickel ain't worth a dime anymore.

If you don't know where you're going, you might end up someplace else.

The future ain't what it used to be.

Always go to other people's funerals. Otherwise, they won't come to yours.

Never answer anonymous letters.

Nobody goes there anymore because it's so crowded.

It ain't over till it's over.

Half the lies they tell about me aren't true.

A guy runs into a bar and says, "Quick, pour me five shots of your best scotch."
The bartender pours the drinks and the man throws them down as fast as he can.
"Wow, that's the fastest drinking I've ever seen," says the bartender.
"Well, you'd drink that fast if you had what I have."
"Well, what do you have?" he asked.
"Fifty cents."

I may be schizophrenic but at least I have each other.

I'd tell you to go to hell, but I work there and I don't want to see you every day.

The best way to remember your wife's birthday. Forget it once.

An airline introduced a special package for businessmen. Buy your ticket and your wife's ticket is free. After great success, the company sent letters to all the wives asking them how the trip was.
The all gave the same reply...WHAT TRIP?

Police came to my house earlier and said my dog had chased someone on a bike I said, "You must be joking, officer, my dog hasn't got a bike."

Why do I have to press 1 for English when you're going to transfer me to someone I can't understand anyway?

How does a spoiled rich girl change a light bulb?
Asks Daddy for a new apartment!

There are 3 kinds of men in the world: Some remain single and make wonders happen. Some have girlfriends and see wonders happen. The rest get married and wonder...
What the hell happened?

Why don't Jewish mothers drink?
Alcohol interferes with their suffering.

Summary of every Jewish holiday:
They tried to kill us, we won, let's eat.

A SHORT HISTORY OF MEDICINE

2,000 B.C.: "Here, eat this compound of root."
200 A.D.: "Don't touch that root. It's the work of the devil. Pray to get better."
1850 A.D.: "Prayer will not help. Take this potion."
1940 A.D.: "That potion is no better than snake oil. Take this pill instead."
1950 A.D: "Take this course of antibiotics."
TODAY: "We've found that antibiotics just make germs stronger. Here, eat this compound of root."

If a lawyer and an IRS agent were drowning, and you could save only one of them, would you read the paper or go to lunch?

A guy asks his buddy, "Have you heard the latest joke about the White House?"

The friend replies, "I happen to work at the White House."
"That's okay. I'll tell it very slowly."

Animal testing is futile. They always get nervous and give the wrong answers!

The Harvard School of Medicine did a study of why Jewish women like Chinese food so much. The study revealed that the reason For this is that because Won Ton spelled backwards is Not Now.

There is a big controversy on the Jewish view of when life begins. In Jewish tradition, the fetus is not considered viable until it graduates from Medical School.

Why do Jewish divorces cost so much?
They're worth it.

Why do Jewish men die before their wives?
They want to.

Why do Jewish mothers make great Parole Officers?
They never let anyone finish a sentence.

What's the difference between a Rottweiler and a Jewish mother?
Eventually, the Rottweiler lets go.

If you want to catch a squirrel, just climb a tree and act like a nut!

Officer to driver going the wrong way on a one way street: "And where do you think you're going?"
Driver: "I'm not sure, but I must be late because everyone else is coming back."

I was feeling very depressed, so I called the ISIS Suicide Hotline. They asked me, "What vest size are you?"

- R. Spaide

Appreciate me now and avoid the rush.

Wife: "What are you doing?"
Husband: "Nothing."
Wife: "Nothing…? You've been reading our marriage certificate for an hour.
"I was looking for the expiration date."

Suicidal twin kills her sister by mistake.

The reasons Politicians work so hard to get re-elected is that they would hate to have to make a living under the laws they passed.

We all love to spend money buying new clothes, but we never realize that the best moments in life are enjoyed without clothes.

Abstinence leaves a lot to be desired.

I don't mind going to work. But the eight hour wait to go home is a bitch.

Arguing over a woman's bust size is like choosing between Budweiser, Rolling Rock, Molson and Heineken. Men may state their preferences, but will grab whatever is available.

It's not whether you win or lose, but how you place the blame.

Having a cold drink on a hot day with a few friends is nice, but having a hot friend on a cold night after a few drinks is priceless.

We have enough youth. How about a fountain of smart?

A fool and his money can throw a heck of a party.

The original point and click interface was a Smith & Wesson.

A wise man once said.....go ask a woman.

Artificial intelligence is no match for natural stupidity.

Bitchery – The art of pissing people off while smiling sweetly.

Does anyone get road rage from pushing a cart in Wal-mart?

You know why a banana is like a politician? He comes in-- and first he is green, then he turns yellow and the he is rotten.

My people skills are just fine. It's my tolerance for idiots that needs work.

After a woman is pregnant, all her friends touch her stomach and say "congratulations."
None of them come and touch the man's penis and say "good job."
Talk about double standards!

I do have flabby thighs, but fortunately, my stomach covers them.

It is more comfortable to cry in a Corvette than on a bicycle.

Many people are alive only because it's illegal to shoot them.

If you help someone when they're in trouble, they will remember you when they are in trouble again.

Alcohol does not solve any problems, but then again, neither does milk.

Khakis; what you need to start the car in Boston.

Did you know that dolphins are so smart that within a few weeks of captivity they can train people to stand on the edge of a pool and throw them fish?

The only reason that I would take up walking is that I could hear heavy breathing again.

Every time I hear the dirty word exercise, I have to wash my mouth out with chocolate.

I have to walk early in the morning before my brain figures out what I'm doing.

Xerox and Wurlitzer have plans to merge to produce reproductive organs.

Partners help each other undress before sex, however, after sex they always dress on their own.

Alabama state motto:
"AT LEAST WE'RE NOT MISSSISSIPPI."

If at first you don't succeed, skydiving is not for you.

The latest survey shows that three out of four people make up 75% of the population.

99% of all lawyers give the rest a bad name.

We are born naked, wet and hungry. Then things get worse.

Learn from your parents' mistakes- use birth control.

Money isn't everything, but it sure keeps the kids in touch.

My wife said "Watcha doing today""
I said "Nothing."
She said "You did that yesterday."
I said "I wasn't finished."

Every time I start thinking about how I look, I just find a bar with a happy hour and by the time I leave, I look just fine.

The advantage of exercising every day is so when you die, they'll say, "Well, he looks good, doesn't he."

If you're going to start cross country skiing, start with a small country.

A new Johns Hopkins study has found that women who carry a little extra weight live longer than the men who mention it.

Sometimes in the morning while drinking my coffee, I think about all the people I'm going to piss off today and I smile.

We all get heavier as we get older because there's a lot more information in our heads.

I tried something new today – sodoku toilet paper. All I could come up with were 1s and 2s.

I named my dog "Five Miles" so I can tell people I walk five miles every day.

A dog accepts you as his boss...A cat wants to see your resume.

My wife asked me to see things from a woman's point of view... So I looked out the kitchen window.

The most common sexual position for married couples is doggie style. The husband sits up and begs, and the wife rolls over and plays dead.

Me and my recliner go way back.

Experts predict that one day computers will replace paper altogether. They've obviously forgot about toilet paper.

A man called his mother in Florida.
"Mom, how are you?" he asked.
"Not too good," said the mother. "I've been very weak."
The son said "Why are you weak?"
She said, "Because I haven't eaten in 6 days."
The son said, "That's terrible. Why haven't you eaten for so long?"
The mother replied, "Because I didn't want my mouth to be full in case you should call."

A bum walked up to a Jewish mother on the street and said, "Lady I haven't eaten in three days." "Force yourself," she replied.

Have you seen the new Jewish-American horror movie? It's called "Debbie Does Dishes."

Patient: "I have a ringing in my ears."
Doctor: "Don't answer."

Borrow money from pessimists... they don't expect it back

I don't think my wife likes me very much. When I had a heart attack she wrote for an ambulance.

UNDENIABLE FACTS

A girl is said to be grown up when she starts wearing a bra. A boy is grown up when he starts removing it.

I'm not fat, I'm just easy to see.

One can conclude with reasonable certainty that while hard work and knowledge will get you close, and attitude will get you there, it's the bullshit and ass kissing that will put you over the top.

A monastery decided to start a fish and chips shop. When the store opened a client comes in and asks one of the clerics: "Are you the fish fryer?"
"Oh no", the cleric answers, "I'm the chip monk."

Why is crabgrass crabby? After all, it's winning!

A newly married man asked his wife. "Would you have married me if my father hadn't left me a fortune?"
"Honey," the wife replied sweetly. "I'd have married you no matter who left you a fortune."

A wife asked her husband: "What do you like most about me—my pretty face or my sexy body?"
He looked at her from head to toe and replied, "I like your sense of humor."

If you're wrong and you shut up, you're wise. If you're right and you shut up, you're married.

A husband and wife had a terrible fight. The wife called up her mother and said, "He fought with me again, I'm coming to live with you." The mother said, "He must pay for this! I am coming to live with you!"

Do you believe in love at first sight, or do I have to walk by you again?

Father: "Son when Abraham Lincoln was your age he walked 12 miles to school." Son: "Dad, when Abraham Lincoln was your age, he was President."

Having false teeth – that'll denture confidence.

I submitted 10 puns to a contest to see which one would win.
Sadly, no pun in ten did.

A man goes to a housewarming party.
He turns up the thermostat then leaves.

A farmer was counting his cows and initially only counted 196, but when he rounded them up he had 200.

I wanted to learn to drive a stick shift, but I couldn't find a manual.

My wife is a sex object. Every time I ask for sex, she objects.

I tried to be a taxi driver but I quit. I couldn't stand people talking behind my back.

Not a single person is in a relationship.

One Tequila, Two Tequila, Three Tequila...floor.

If man evolved from monkeys and apes, why do we still have monkeys and apes?

I went to a bookstore and asked the saleswoman where the self-help books were. She said that would defeat the purpose.

Is there another word for synonym?

If the police arrest a mute do they tell him he has the right to remain silent?

How do they get deer to cross the road only at those yellow signs?

Why do they put braille on the drive through bank machines?

One nice thing about egoists—they don't talk about themselves.

Do infants enjoy infancy as much as adults enjoy adultery?

How is it possible to have a civil war?

If one synchronized swimmer drowns, do the rest drown also?

Why is there an expiration date on sour cream?

If you try to fail and succeed which have you done?

Why are hemorrhoids called hemorrhoids instead of "assteroids?"

All we ever do is ask questions? Why?

Would a fly without wings be called a walk?

Be a team player, it spreads out the blame.

If you spin an Oriental man is a circle four times, does he become disoriented?

Can an atheist get insurance against acts of God?

Why do stores have signs that say "Guide dogs only?" The dogs can't read and their owners are blind.

Police: "Knock, knock."
Answer: "Who is it?"
Police: "Police!
Answer: "What do you want?"
Police: "To talk."
Answer: "How many are you?"
Police: "Two."
Answer: "Talk to each other."

A Roman walks into a bar holds up five fingers and says five beers please. A limbo champion walks into a bar and loses his title.

Dear Mother-in law: Don't teach me how to handle my children, I'm living with one of yours and he needs a lot of improvement.

My wife said she wanted to see *50 Shades of Grey.* So I took a photo of her hair.

A Husband was throwing darts at his wife's picture. All were missing the target. Suddenly he received a call from his wife. She says, "Hi, what are you doing?" His honest reply: "Missing you."

God promised men that good and obedient wives would be found in all corners of the world. Then he made the world round... and laughed and laughed.

Adam and Eve had an ideal marriage, He didn't have to hear about all the men she could have married, and she didn't have to hear about his mother's cooking.

You know it's time to use mouthwash when the dentist leaves the room and sends in a canary.

You really do not understand something unless you can explain it to your grandmother.   – Albert Einstein

Liberals can understand everything but people who don't understand them.

My wife handed me two kayak paddles and asked, "which one do you want?" I said I'd take either oar.

Don't drink and drive, it will spill everywhere.

It is true that alcohol kills people, but how many are born because of it?

I was married by a judge. I should have asked for a jury.

I never forget a face, but in your case I'll be glad to make an exception.

A black cat crossing your path signifies that the animal is going somewhere.

From the moment I picked your book up until I laid it down I was convulsed with laughter.
Someday I intend to read it.

A man's got to believe in something. I believe I'll have another drink.

Drive carefully. Uncle Sam needs every taxpayer he can get.

He may look like an idiot and talk like an idiot but don't let that fool you. He really is an idiot.

Beauty is in the eye of the beer-holder.

Congress has solved the problem of how to get the people to pay taxes they can't afford for services they don't need.

Don't look now, but there's one too many people in this room and I think it's you.

There was a time when $1,000.00 was the down payment on a car. Now it's the sales tax.

Alcohol is never the answer... But it does make you forget the question!

Behind every successful man is a woman. Behind this woman is his wife.

Age is not a particularly interesting subject. Anyone can get old... all you have to do is live long enough.

When life hands you lemons, find some tequila and salt!

Those are my principles. If you don't like them I have others.

My doctor told me to watch my drinking. Now I drink in front of the mirror.

Who are you going to believe? Me or your lyin' eyes?

Women should be obscene and not heard. Relationship has 12 letters. But then again, so does "Time For Shots."

I don't make mistakes, I date them.

Time flies like an arrow. Fruitflies like a banana.

Golf is a lot like taxes. You drive hard to get to the green and then wind up in the hole.

Some things are better left unsaid. I'll probably get drunk and say them anyway.

Time wounds all heels.

The husband who wants a happy marriage should keep his mouth shut and his checkbook open.

She got her good looks from her father. He's a plastic surgeon.

America is the land of opportunity. Everybody can become a taxpayer.

Quote me as saying I was mis-quoted.

Why does a chicken coop have two doors? If it had four it would be a chicken sedan.

Why did the author write his novel in the basement? He wanted to write a best-seller.

Politics is the art of looking for trouble, finding it, misdiagnosing it and then misapplying the wrong remedies.

My body is not a temple. It is a distillery with legs.

Politics doesn't make strange bedfellows. Marriage does.

Remember men, you are fighting for your lady's honor. Which is probably more than she ever did.

Last night I shot an elephant in my pajamas. How he got in my pajamas I will never know!

A lady walked into a store and asked the sales lady if she could try on a cute dress in the window. The saleslady replied: "Sure, but wouldn't you be more comfortable in the dressing room?"

Nostalgia isn't what it used to be.

What do I care about posterity? What's posterity ever done for me?

I worked myself up from nothing to a state of extreme poverty.

If you want to see a comic strip, you should see me in the shower.

I made a killing on Wall Street. A few years ago I shot my broker.

Confucius says: "Men who drink beer all day have wet dreams all night."

I'm not an alcoholic. Alcoholics go to meetings. If I'm drunk, I go to parties.

Money talks. All mine says is "goodbye."

Here's to our wives and girlfriends! May they never meet.

I've had a wonderful evening. But this wasn't it.

Now there's a man with an open mind! You can feel the breeze from here!

Room service? Send up a larger room!

If I held you any closer I would be on the other side of you!

I chased a girl around for two years, only to discover that her tastes were exactly like mine: we both were crazy about girls!

Alcohol doesn't make you fat. It makes you lean... on chairs, tables and other people.

I must say that television is very educational. The minute someone turns it on, I go to the library and read a book!

A man's only as good as the woman he feels.

I'm not an alcoholic. Alcoholics need a drink. I already have one.

Either this man is dead or my watch has stopped.

I used to feel like a man trapped in a woman's body, but then I got born

Father: Don't you think our son gets his brains from me?
Mother: Probably, dear. I still have all of mine.

Nothing makes a person more modest about their income than filling out a tax return.

I don't recycle because it would make me seem like a huge alcoholic to my garbage-man.

I sent the club a message to accept my resignation. I don't care to belong to any club that will have me as a member!

I'm not feeling well, and need a doctor immediately! Call the nearest golf course!

I wish to be cremated. One tenth of my ashes shall be given to my agent, as written in our contract.

You know what's fun about being sober? Nothing.

Income tax is the fine you pay for thriving so fast!

I don't have a photograph, but you can have my footprints. They're upstairs in my socks.

George Washington never told a lie, but then again he never had to file a form 1040.

What did the man with a slab of asphalt under his arm order? A beer, please and one for the road!

What is an astronaut's favorite key on a keyboard? The spacebar!

Why did God invent Jameson whiskey? So the Irish would never rule the world!

In 1913, Uncle Sam only collected $13 million in income taxes. That's why they were called "the good old days!"

Eskimos eat whale meat and blubber. I'd blubber too if I had to eat whale meat.

My girlfriend was telling me that obesity was in her genes. I told her that can't be true... she looked fat in that skirt as well!

Getting hit in the balls is more painful than giving birth. Proof: guys don't want to be hit in the balls, but women want to give birth!

My fat wife started crying because the airline made her book two seats. I said, "Yes, but you'll get two meals!" That cheered her right up.

A bee went into a bar and left an hour later buzzing.

Star Wars: a very long time ago, but somehow still in the future.

I went to an Italian restaurant, and they had spaghetti and meatballs on the menu. So I had to call the waiter to wipe it off.

What do you say when you're drunk and call someone up? Al-cohol you!

Man to woman: "Have you ever had sex?" Woman: "That's my business." Man: "Ah, a professional!"

It's annoying when people say that obesity runs in their family. Clearly nothing runs in their family.

What's an astronaut's favorite candy? A mars bar!

Despite being on the contraceptive pill, my girlfriend keeps getting pregnant. I might as well just not bother taking them!

I don't understand fast food. I've been eating it for years, and I just keep getting slower!

I hate when I wish on a star only to realize it was just an airplane.

Why don't politicians drink? It interferes with their suffering!

Hospitality: making your guests feel like they're at home, when in reality you wish they were home... at their house!

Many people are worried about the effects of genetically-modified foods. "There is no proof of any adverse effects," said one carrot.

What do blondes and a bottle of Corona have in common? They are both empty from the neck up!

I married a girl who said she didn't believe in sex before marriage. In hindsight, I should have made sure that she believed in sex after marriage.

How do you find a man in a bar who is sensitive, listens and is sweet? Look for any man drinking a Mike's Hard Lemonade.

Why doesn't anyone like the restaurant on the moon? Because it has no atmosphere.

The wife said she's sick of me 'always being right.' So I left.

They should ban semi-colons; no one knows how to use them.

The bank says that this is my final notice. Isn't it fantastic that they're not going to bother me anymore?

My girlfriend told me that when she runs her hands over her body, she feels lumps of fat that piss her off. I said, 'I know how you feel.'

I'm not the jealous type. I wish I was, though.

Do cross-eyed teachers have trouble controlling their pupils?

If it weren't for marriage, men would spend their lives thinking they had no faults at all.

Filing a tax return can be defined as self-inflicted mugging.

What do you call a tick on the moon? A lunatic!

My dog was getting tired of not getting fed. Then he died.

The most important thing in a relationship is trust. If you don't trust your girlfriend, how do you know she's not going to tell your wife?

I kicked the kid downstairs in the face because I thought he was spying on my wife. Turns out he just got a new trampoline.

A reporter interviewed a millionaire and asked what he was before getting married. He replied, 'A billionaire.'

What did the alien say to the cat? "Take me to your litter."

The best tax law is the one that gets the most feathers with the least squawking.

How do fat chance and slim chance mean the same thing?

Why did the cow jump over the moon? The farmer had cold hands!

What do a near-sighted gynecologist and a puppy have in common? A wet nose.

My wife and I decided to make a sex tape. She was angry when I started holding auditions for her part.

Two gypsy fortune-tellers meet on the street. One says to the other: "You're fine. How am I?"

My wife said I'm a useless, lazy slob and that she deserves much better. I replied, "You woke me up at 3 P.M. just to tell me that?"

I got in the car with my drug dealer the other day. He drove around slowly for a while before picking up speed.

I was going through airport customs when security asked me if I had any firearms. Apparently "What do you need?" was the wrong answer.

If anyone steals my identity, at least I'll know who to look out for.

If you stand by the sea, it sounds like putting a shell to your ear!

One of the most difficult things in the world is trying to convince a woman that even a bargain costs money.

How long a minute is depends on what side of the bathroom door you're on.

A dog's bark may be worse than its bite, but everyone prefers the bark.

My wife said I'm full of my own self-importance. Anyway... that's enough about her.

Two blondes in Las Vegas were sitting in a bar chatting, when one asked the other, "Which do you think is farther away... Florida or the moon?"
The other blonde turned to her friend and said, "Hellooooo, can you see Florida?!"

After it's all said and done, the politicians say it and the tax payers do it.

Where do astronauts grab a drink? At the spacebar!

I heard rumors that my wife was having sex behind an Italian restaurant. I wouldn't put it pasta.

My dad used to say that honesty was the best policy, which was ironic coming from the man who told me about Santa, the Easter Bunny and the Tooth Fairy.

Does Satan get a lot of letters from dyslexic kids at Christmas?

What's worse than finding a fly in your soup? A vein in your hot dog.

Parallel lines have got so much in common.

I like to sleep with the bedside lamp on, even though my wife feels that it's weird. I don't see why – I think it makes a great hat.

Giraffes look down on people like you.

If you are supposed to learn from your mistakes, why do some people have more than one child?

I tried looking up the definition of 'opaque' today. It was not very clear.

My wife complained that I never lift a finger around the house. So I did: the middle one.

Exaggeration is a billion times worse than understatement.

I said to the pharmacist, 'I need some condoms.' She said, 'Just a minute.' I said 'Yes, those are the ones.'

I fell down a really deep, dark hole today. I couldn't see that well.

I was just about to nail some shelves to the wall. Then I thought, screw it.

Never trust a man sitting in a wheelchair with dirty shoes.

When my wife refuses to have sex with me, I just take matters into my own hand.

Plagiarism: getting in trouble for something you didn't do.

I was an accountant from age twenty to age thirty, when I was fired for no apparent reason. What a waste of fourteen years.

My wife and I were arguing one night, when she said 'You'll drive me to my grave!' I had the car out in thirty seconds.

I've often wanted to drown my troubles, but I can't get my wife to go swimming.

I've just published a book on preserving the rainforest from deforestation. It's over 2,000 pages long.

My hamster died from lack of exercise. He just didn't have the wheel to live.

Two cannibals are eating a clown.
One turns to the other and says,
"Hey, does this taste funny to you?"

A dyed-in-the wool patriot is one who says he sorry he has only one income to give to his country.

What should be in a book to make it a bestseller? A girl on the cover, nut no cover on the girl!

When I was a teenager, I had sex almost every day. Almost on a Monday, almost on a Tuesday...

Behind every successful man stand a woman and the IRS. One takes the credit and the other takes the cash.

I was in bed with a blind girl last night and she said I had the biggest penis she'd ever laid her hands on. I said to her, "You're pulling my leg."

My girlfriend thinks I'm a stalker. Well, she's not exactly my girlfriend yet.

If at first you don't succeed, destroy all evidence that you tried.

I went for my routine check-up today and everything seemed fine until the guy stuck his finger up my butt! Do you think I should change dentists?

My wife had been missing over a week, and the police told me to prepare for the worst. So I went back to the secondhand store to get all of her clothes back.

I was explaining to my wife last night that when you die, you get reincarnated but must come back as a different creature. She said she would like to come back as a cow. I said that she was obviously not listening.

A wife of an elderly couple says to her husband "You're always pushing me around and talking behind my back." The husband says, "What do you expect? You're in a wheelchair!"

I had amnesia once. Okay, maybe twice.

All I ask is a chance to prove that money won't make me happy.

I saw a poor old lady fall over today on the sidewalk. At least I presume she was poor... she only had $1.20 in her purse!

If the world were a logical place, men would be the ones who ride horses sidesaddle.

What is a "free gift?" Shouldn't all gifts be free?

They told me I was gullible and I believed them.

Teach a child to be polite and courteous in the home and when he grows up he'll never be able to merge his car onto the freeway.

Experience is the one thing you have left when everything else is gone.

One nice thing about egotists: they don't talk about other people.

Girl: What color are my eyes? Guy: 34C

If swimming is so good for your figure, then how do you explain whales?

Is it just me, or do Buffalo wings taste like chicken?

I decided not to be pessimistic. It wouldn't work anyway.

If a man sleeps with a lot of women he gets called a stud. If a woman sleeps with a lot of men she gets called a lot.

ANONYMOUS JOKES BY RICK SPAIDE

I always try to keep a low profile. I figured I had to get out there a little more at some point, so I went to Anonymous Anonymous. At the first meeting I got up and said, "Hello, my name is, well... don't worry about it."

Once I went to Paranoids Anonymous. I got up in front and said, "Why are you people looking at me?"

I went to Hypochondriacs Anonymous and said, "Hello my name is Rick and I have all the problems."

I went to Halitosis Anonymous. I got up front and said, "Why are all of you sitting so far back?"

What do they serve at Coffee Drinkers Anonymous?

I've joined Alcoholics Anonymous. I still drink but I use a false name.

PHYLLIS DILLERISMS

Whatever you may look like, marry a man your own age. As your beauty fades, so will his eyesight.

Housework can't kill you, but why take the chance?

Cleaning your house while your kids are still growing is like shoveling the sidewalk before it stops snowing.

The reason women don't play football is because 11 of them would never wear the same outfit in public.

Best way to get rid of kitchen odors: eat out.

A bachelor is a guy who never made the same mistake once.

I want my children to have all the things I couldn't afford. Then I want to move in with them.

Most children threaten at times to run away from home. This is the only thing that keeps some parents going.

We spend the first twelve months of our children's lives teaching them to walk and talk and the next twelve years telling them to sit down and shut up.

Burt Reynolds once asked me out. I was in his room.

What I don't like about Christmas parties is looking for a job the next day.

My photographs don't do me justice. They just look like me.

I admit I have a tremendous sex drive. My boyfriend lives forty miles away.

Tranquilizers work only if you follow the advice on the bottle – keep away from children.

I asked the waiter "Is this milk fresh?" He said, "Lady, three hours ago it was grass."

The reason the golf pro tells you to keep your head down is so you can't see him laughing.

You know you're old if they have discontinued your blood type.

ON THE IRS AND TAXES

It is reported that the politicians in Washington are thinking of abolishing the income tax and simply taking the income.

A lot of people save the first dollar they ever made. Uncle Sam has all the others.

A politician is a man who never met a tax he didn't try to hike.

After all is said and done, the politicians say it and the taxpayers do it.

Regardless of who wins an election, they have to raise taxes to pay for the damage.

Poverty is what you experience the day after paying taxes.

The way the cost of living and taxes are today, you might as well marry for love.

The average man lives thirty-five years longer than he did in 1850.
Well, he has to these days in order to get his taxes paid!

Stay on your job and pay your taxes promptly. Thousands of workers at the IRS are depending on you.

The reward for saving money is being able to pay our taxes without borrowing.

At no time is it easier to keep your mouth shut than on an audit of your tax returns.

If there are no ups and downs in your life, you're dead!

You really can't beat the game. If you earn anything, it's minus taxes. If you buy anything, it's plus taxes.

We wonder why they call it a "tax return," when so little of the money does.

Did you ever notice that when you put the words "The" and "IRS" together, it spells "Theirs?"

Death and taxes are inevitable, but death doesn't repeat itself.

A rancher asked his veterinarian for some advice.
"I have a horse that walks normally some days, and other days it limps. What should I do?"
The vet replied: "The next time he walks normally, sell him."

"I've never flown in a plane before," said an old woman to the pilot. "You will bring me down safely, won't you?"
"All I can say ma'am," said the pilot, "is that I've never left anyone up there yet!"

We don't need a dinner bell in our house. We have a smoke alarm.

I wonder how things worked out for that guy who grabbed the bull by the horns.

I got home from work and found my wife on a porn site. I'll have to speak to her about that when she gets home.

If smoking kills, why does it cure salmon?

I read somewhere that humans only use 10% of their brains. I wonder what the other half is for.

I went on holiday to China and bought a pair of shoes. I looked on the sole and it said, "Made around the corner."

I worry about germs on money. So I try to spend it before it makes me sick.

The wife was looking very pleased with herself today. She's found something that still fits from her schooldays – a pair of earrings.

When we got married, she treated me like a god. As the years went by, the letters got reversed.

My wife said we need to communicate more. So I sent her my email address.

Judge: I thought I told you I never wanted to see you again.
Criminal: That's what I told the police, but they wouldn't listen.

I used to be part of a band called "Missing Cat." You probably saw our posters.

I think I'm going to order a load of bubble wrap just to see what it's packed in.

I'm the kind of guy who stops the microwave with one second to go, just to feel like a bomb defuser.

Don't abuse alcohol, drink it.

Wife: Are you having an affair?
Husband: I'm not going to stand here and lie to you.
...so he sat down and lied to her instead!

My wife is a magician. She can turn anything into an argument.

Who wants to be a millionaire? Everyone except billionaires.

I just spent half an hour trying to take my wife's bra off – I wish I had never tried it on.

I've discovered why women ask so many questions. They have an extra why chromosome.

People who say they sleep like a baby usually don't have one.

Treat each day as your last; one day you will be right.

The only honest people in the world are small children and drunk people.

I don't see the point in testing cosmetics on rabbits. Aren't they cute enough as it is?

Better late than pregnant.

Ballerinas always dance on their tip-toes, which makes me wonder... why not just hire taller girls?

I was in a spelling bee once. But I lost because the other students cheeted.

I work as a waiter. Pay isn't great but I put food on the table.

The future is much like the present, only longer.

If it's your birthday in November, you know your parents really enjoyed Valentine's Day.

I said to my wife, "I've found this amazing new lipstick that helps you lose weight!" It was a disguised tube of superglue.

Unfortunately, I have one pair of running shoes and sixteen pairs of eating shoes.

I gave blood today. I know it's not the best gift to give on Valentine's day, but it came from the heart.

I'd like to thank the person who looked at a buzzing beehive and thought, "those bastards are hiding something delicious here, I just know it!"

One day, my girlfriend sent me a text saying we should break up. I didn't even have time to be sad because she sent me another text a few moments later saying "Sorry, wrong person."

I went for a job interview today and the boss asked me, "Why did you leave your last job?" I said, "The company relocated and didn't tell me where."

I made a chicken salad last night.
Apparently they prefer to eat grain.

Yoga class is great. You can close your eyes
and imagine yourself in a relaxing place.
Like on your sofa, not doing yoga.

I'm not fat! I'm just so sexy it's overflowing.

If vegetarians love animals so much, why do
they eat all the animal's food?

Smoke detectors need to be tested from
time to time. So sometimes I cook .

There was a piece of cake in the fridge with
a note on it saying, "Don't eat me." Now
there's an empty plate and a note that reads
"I don't take orders from a cake."

Do guns have a troubleshooting section?

Rubbish: the stuff you throw away.
Stuff: the rubbish you keep.

Jail: the government's way of sending you to
your room.

My girlfriend dumped me because she thought I was always one step ahead of her. My response: "Your bags are in the car."

A blind mad walks into a bar. And a table. And a chair.

Last night I tried to go to out for an Italian meal, but there was a huge fat woman in the doorway. I couldn't get pasta.

Do women shake the gas pump after filling the tank, or is that just a man thing?

Him: I'd go through anything for you.
Her: The door would be nice.

Some guy just gave me half of a peace sign.

I've installed a skylight in my apartment. The people who live above me are furious.

I'm at a point in my life where enjoying lots of bars just means a good phone signal.

How do trespassers get in your home? Intruder window.

Do not underestimate me. That's my family's job.

Not many people knew that Albert Einstein had a brother who was experimented on by a mad scientist. His name was Frank Einstein.

I've not been to work in four days. I've almost forgotten how to play solitaire and minesweeper.

I've done 100 pull-ups. This new belt is terrible.

I knew I was going bald when it kept taking longer and longer to wash my face.

Just got the results of my MRI scan back and I've been diagnosed with Brian. It's a brain disorder.

I'm very suspicious about joggers. They're always the ones who find the bodies.

Why it that a woman only believes what a man says when it's a compliment?

If you want your spouse to listen and pay strict attention to every word you say, talk in your sleep.

I can beat anybody in a fight with one hand. It's the two-handed guys who beat the crap out of me.

I got sent out of class once at school. The teacher yelled at me, saying "What would your parents say if I called them?" I replied, "Hello?"

What's the difference between ignorance and apathy? I don't know and I don't care.

I hate being bipolar. It's amazing.

You know you're ugly when you're always the one asked to take the photo.

The kids will be mad when they discover that there is no law that prohibits them from talking while I drive.

I just put in some earplugs and had a near-deaf experience.

The first rule of the Procrastination Club: I'll tell you later.

Did you hear the one about the scarecrow winning the Nobel Prize? He was outstanding in his field.

The healthiest part of the doughnut is the hole. Too bad you have to eat around it to get there!

Facebook is like jail. You sit around and waste time, write on walls and get poked by people you don't know.

My therapist says that I am socially awkward because I misunderstand what people mean. I'm pretty sure she wants me.

If your doctor warns that you have to watch your drinking, find a bar with a mirror.

Leadership is about making bold decisions even when you have no idea what anyone in the meeting is talking about.

Laugh at your problems, everyone else does.

If sex with three people is called a threesome and sex with two people is called a twosome, I now understand why they call you handsome.

If people were meant to pop out of bed first thing in the morning, we would all sleep on toasters.

A real problem drinker is the guy who never buys.

Always remember you're unique – just like everyone else.

They call our first language our mother-tongue because our fathers never got the chance to speak!

If we're not supposed to eat animals, then why are they made out of meat?

If you are what you eat, then my dog is a newspaper.

A friend of mine has a trophy wife, but apparently he didn't get first place.

Humble and proud of it.

Little did he know, but that never stopped him.

My boss put up a "conserve energy" sign at the office. I guess I better put my feet up and nap for a while.

Sometimes I make a mental note and forget where I put it.

I met the girl of my dreams last night. Then I woke up.

Mistakes are proof that you're trying. And incompetent.

I am at my most photogenic when the photos are of someone else.

Wisdom doesn't always come with age. Sometimes age just shows up by itself.

I think it's wrong that only one company makes the game Monopoly. – Steven Wright

The last time someone told me I looked hot it was 100 degrees outside.

If two people love each other, nothing is impossible. Except deciding where to eat.

Be careful of your thoughts. They may become your words at any moment.

If a firefighter's business can go up in flames and a plumber's business can go down the drain, then can a hooker get laid off?

I feel like we've met before. It must be a case of déjà who!

I'd be such a great womanizer if I could only get the women to look at me!

I like to sugar-coat my words because I know I'll inevitably end up eating them.

Technically, all breakfasts are continental unless you eat them in the ocean.

Technically, a slippery slope is also the path of least resistance.

I have a hidden talent. I wish I could find it.

A true pessimist will look at a glass filled with water and say that the glass is too small.

Promises are a bit like babies: fun to make, but hard to deliver.

I like to have dessert first, then the main dish and finish with the appetizer. Does that mean I have an eating disorder?

My mother was so overprotective that we were only permitted to play rock, paper.

I gave my wife plastic surgery by cutting up her credit cards.

I am fairly certain that I could be arrested any day now for being a serial time killer.

How doe Moses make his tea?
Hebrews it...

Venison for dinner again? Oh deer!

A cartoonist was found dead in his home. Details are sketchy.

I used to be a banker, but then I lost interest.

Atheism is a non-prophet organization.

Haunted French pancakes give me the crepes.

They told me I had type A blood, but that was a typ-o.

Jokes about German sausages are the wurst.

I stayed up all night to see where the sun went, but then it dawned on me.

When the chemists die, they barium.

This girl said that she knew me from the vegetarian club, but I'd never met herbivore.

I'm reading a book about anti-gravity chambers. I just can't put it down!

I did a theatrical performance about puns. It was a play on words.

I didn't like my beard at first, but then it grew on me.

Did you hear the one about the cross-eyed teacher who lost her job because she couldn't control her pupils?

When you get a bladder infection, you know urine trouble.

Broken pencils are pretty much pointless.

What do you call a dinosaur with an extensive vocabulary? A thesaurus!

I dropped out of a class on Communism because of lousy Marx.

I got a job at a bakery because I kneaded dough!

I read recipes the same way I read science fiction. I get to the end and I think, "Well, that's not going to happen!"

The other night I ate at a family restaurant. Every table had an argument going.

Never marry a man who was captain of the debating team.

Have you ever noticed that everyone seems to have a camcorder these days, and no one talks about seeing UFOs like they used to?

According to a recent survey, men say that the first thing they notice about a woman is her eyes. Women say that the first thing they notice about men is that they're a bunch of liars.

When I feel blue, I start breathing again.

In the 1960s, people took acid to make the world look weird. Now the world is weird and people take Prozac to make it seem normal.

Politics is supposed to be the second-oldest profession. I have come to realize that it bears very little resemblance to the first.

How is it that one match can start a forest fire, but it takes a whole box to start a campfire?

Getting married is like getting into the bathtub. After a while, it ain't so hot.

A girl walks into a supermarket and asks the clerk, "Can I have some turkey for my grandma?" The clerk responded, "Sorry. We don't do exchanges."

I got an offer for a credit card with a year with no interest. Just like my life.

Bisexuality immediately doubles your chances for a date on a Saturday night

My mother never saw the irony of calling me a son-of-a-bitch.   –Jack Nicholson

Sometimes the first step to forgiveness is realizing the other person was born an idiot.

Telling a girl to calm down works about as well as trying to baptize a cat.

Why can't women learn to read maps? Only the male mind can comprehend the concept of one inch equals a mile.

What are the worst six years in a blonde's life? Third grade.

They say you are what you eat, so lay off the nuts.

It used to be only death and taxes were inevitable. Now there's also shipping and handling.

Olympic track makes you feel like you witnessed a crime, because you hear a gunshot and then see a bunch of guys running.

I think sex is better than logic but I can't prove it.

If someone hates you for no reason, give that bastard a reason.

Never break someone's heart because they only have one...break their bones instead.

I don't think you act stupid, I'm sure it's the real thing.

Your family tree must be a cactus because everybody on it is a prick

Intelligence is like underwear. It's important that you have it, but not necessary that you show it off.

Anger: the feeling that makes your mouth work faster than your mind.

Why is there so much blood in my alcohol system?

Where do they get the seeds for seedless watermelons?

Why do people keep running over a thread with their vacuum cleaners, then reach down, examine it then put it down in order to give the vacuum one more chance?

I named my hard drive "Dat Ass", so once a month my computer asks if I want to back dat ass up.

Why do Black Widow spiders kill their males after mating? To stop the snoring before it starts.

Change is inevitable, except from a vending machine.

For Sale – Parachute only used once, never opened.

PMS should be called ovary-acting.

We never knew he was a drunk until he came to work sober.

I sometimes watch birds and wonder if I was a bird, who would I shit on.

You were so ugly, when your mom dropped you off for school, she got a fine for littering

What do you call a smart blonde?
A golden retriever.

Thieves have broken into my house and stolen everything except my soap, shower gel deodorant and towels. Dirty Bastards.

Don't forget that alcohol helps to remove the stress, the bra, the panties and many other problems.

Why was Cinderella thrown off the basketball team?
She ran away from the ball.

My five year old: "I don't want to be your daughter anymore! I QUIT!" No two weeks' notice or anything. She'd better not expect a reference.

How do trees access the internet? They log in.

What nails do carpenters hate to hit?
Fingernails!

What is the lightest thing in the world?
A penis - just a thought can lift it!

What is the difference between snowmen and snowwomen?
Snowballs.

When wearing a bikini, women reveal about 90% of their body. Men are polite enough to only look at the covered parts.

I just read that 4,154,867 people were married last year. Not to cause trouble, but shouldn't this be an even number?

HILAROUS ONE LINERS

WORD PLAY

Follow your dreams! (except for that one where you're naked in church)

I'd tell you to go to hell; but I work there and I don't want to have to see you every day.

When your gecko is broken, you have a reptile dysfunction.

I have kleptomania; but when it gets really bad, I just take something for it!

I may be schizophrenic, but at least I have each other.

A bartender is a pharmacist with a limited inventory.

Nobody is perfect. I am a nobody. Therefore, I am perfect.

Money isn't everything, but it sure keeps the kids in touch.

When you work here, you can name your own salary. I call mine Zelda.

I want to die in my sleep like my grandfather, not screaming in terror like the passengers in his car.

Dyslexics have more nuf.

I love cooking with wine. Sometimes I even put it into the food.

I am having an out-of-money experience.

Corduroy pillows are making headlines!

Paula Deen says the N-word in private. Loses her job and is hated by millions. Quentin Tarantino directs a movie that says the N-word 113 times. Wins awards and makes millions. Well played, Tarantino, well played.

I called the Incontinence Hotline...
They asked, "Can you hold, please?"

Two elderly women on a walk with buzzards circling overhead. One says: "I'm not saying we're getting old but I wouldn't stand in one place very long."

A day without sunshine is like, well...night.

A fine is a tax for doing wrong.
A tax is a fine for doing well.

Change is inevitable...except from a vending machine.

When you go to court, you are putting yourself in the hands of twelve people who weren't smart enough to get out of jury duty.

Those who live by the sword get shot by those who don't.

The things that come to those who wait may be the things left by those who got there first.

Light travels faster than sound. This may explain why so many people appear bright until they open their mouths to speak.

Dijon vu: the same mustard as before.

There is a great need for a sarcasm font.

When I was teaching preschool, there were two little girls, best friends, who spent each day being a Disney character. One day I heard one call the other "Alison." I couldn't recall a single Disney character called Alison, so I asked her who she was today. "Alison Wonderland," she replied.

Bad decisions make good stories.

Sometimes, I'll look down at my watch three consecutive times and still not know what time it is.

I totally take back all those times I didn't want to take a nap when I was a kid.

You never know when it will strike, but there comes a moment when you know that you just aren't going to do anything productive for the rest of the day.

When two egotists meet, it's an I for an I.

Condoms should be used on every conceivable occasion.

Shotgun wedding: a case of wife or death.

A hangover is the wrath of grapes.

A bicycle can't stand on its own because it's two-tired.

She was engaged to a boy with a wooden leg but broke it off.

If you don't pay your exorcist... you get repossessed.

When cannibals ate a missionary, they got a taste of religion.

Time flies like an arrow. Fruit flies like a banana.

Bakers trade bread recipes on a knead-to-know basis.

She was only a whisky maker but he loved her still.

No matter how hard you push the envelope, it will still be stationery.

A dog gave birth to puppies near the road and was cited with littering.

A lot of money is tainted. 'Taint yours and 'taint mine.

A boiled egg in the morning is hard to beat.

Once you've seen one shopping center... you've seen a mall.

Acupuncture is a jab well done.

Santa's helpers are subordinate clauses.

I knew a fellow who sent ten puns to friends with the hope that at least one of the puns would make them laugh. No pun in ten did.

WORD PLAY: MEDICAL DIVISION

The AMA has weighed in on the President's Health Care Plan.

Allergists were in favor of scratching it; but the *dermatologists* advised "no rash moves."

Gastroenterologists had a kind of gut feeling about it but the *neurologists* thought the President had a lot of nerve.

Meanwhile, *obstetricians* felt certain that everyone was laboring under a false misconception, while the *ophthalmologists* considered that short-sighted.

The *psychiatrists* thought the whole idea was madness, while the *radiologists* could see right through it.

Surgeons decided to wash their hands of the whole thing and the *internists* agreed that it would be a bitter pill to swallow.

Plastic surgeons figured this proposal would put "a whole new face on the matter;" the *podiatrists* thought it a step forward; but the *urologists* were pissed off at the whole idea.

Anesthesiologists thought it was all a gas; and those high-minded *cardiologists* just didn't have the heart for it.

In the end, the *proctologists* won the day, leaving the entire decision up to the assholes in Washington.

Pathologists yelled, "Over my dead body!" while the *pediatricians* said, "Oh, grow up!"

I didn't make it to the gym today. That's five years in a row.

Shirts get dirty. Underwear gets dirty. Pants? Pants never get dirty, and you can wear them forever.

How many times is it appropriate to say "What?" before you just nod and smile because you still didn't hear or understand a word they said.

I'm always slightly terrified when I exit out of Word and it asks me if I want to save any changes to my ten-page technical report that I swear I did not make any changes to.

A grenade thrown into a kitchen in France would result in linoleum blown apart.

Why pay to have your family tree traced? Go into politics and your opponents will do it for you.

I'm really sorry I hurt your feelings when I called you stupid. I thought you already knew.

Those who say, "There's no such thing as a stupid question," have never worked in Customer Service.

Sometimes you have to burn a few bridges to keep the crazies from following you.

Not to get technical...but according to chemistry, alcohol is a solution.

I disagree with Kay Jewelers. I would bet on any given Friday or Saturday night, more kisses begin with Miller Light than with Kay.

I have a hard time deciphering the fine line between boredom and hunger.

A chicken crossing the road is poultry in motion.

Nothing sucks more than that moment during an argument when you realize you're wrong.

The man who fell into the upholstery machine is fully recovered.

Some people just need a sympathetic pat...
    On the head...
        With a hammer.

I'd be unstoppable, if not for law enforcement and Physics.

Being male is a matter of birth. Being a man is a matter of age. Being a gentleman is a matter of choice.

During a children's church service, the subject was resurrection. One little boy raised his hand and said, "I know that if you have a resurrection that lasts more than four hours, you're supposed to call the doctor." Goes to show you that there are commercials that ought to be muted at home.

It was our second anniversary and my husband sent me flowers to the office. He told the florist to say "It's Year Number Two" on the card. I was thrilled with the bouquet, but not so pleased about the card that read, "Happy Anniversary. You're Number Two."

Homer calls Easy Jet to book a flight. The operator asks, "How many people are flying with you?"
Homer replies: "How should I know? It's your plane!"

You never appreciate what you have 'til it's gone. Toilet paper is a good example.

A set of jumper cables goes into a bar. bartender asks, "What are you doing here?"
They say, "We just want a drink."
He says, "All right, but don't start anything!"

MICHAEL JIRAN'S DEFINITIONS

Mr. Jiran's definitions are humorous definitions of a word or phrase, usually expressed as a pun or other word play (it often helps to read the answer aloud).

A mother or a father (noun) . . . .
APPARENT

Food you give to a gerbil (noun) . . . . .
APPELLATE

Something growing on your colon . . . .
ASSIST

Needed to support a gov't program . . .
ATTACKS

Honey-producing insect living near inlet . .
BABY

Where some dresses end. . . . .
BALONEY

When I want to know about a girl. . . .
ALASKA

Five cents left in a saloon. .. . .
BARNACLE

Said when swatting away a wasp. . . . . .
BELIEVE

Robert will. . . . .
BOBBLE

A jar of lies. . . . .
CANNIBAL

Can't run off and get married.. . . . . . .
CANTELOUPE

A stupid ex-prisoner. .. . .
CONDOM

Against a Middle Eastern ruler. . . . . .
CONSULTANT

What pie apples say. . . . .
CHORUS

A crazy pickle. . . . .
DAFFODIL

Swore at some guy . . . .
CUSTOM

Making a joke about death . . . . . .
DIGEST

Fear of devices that keep you out . .
DREADLOCKS

A trial-holding vessel. . . . .
COURTSHIP

A breath mint eaten inside. . . .
ENDORSEMENT

When team players are same size . .
FARENHEIT

What pigeons say to people . . . . . .
FETUS

A male making gestures . . . .
EMOTIONS

Where Tom Sawyer was often found. . . . . .
FISSION

Why she went shopping . . . .
FORECLOSE

Berliner finished his meal . . . .
GERMINATE

Special floor for baby . . . .
INFANTILE

Coins for a pony . . . .

HORSE SENSE

This container has disappeared . . . .
JARGON

What to say to a round object . . . .
HI BALL

A female deer in the girls' bathroom. . .
JOHN DOE

The coins a pony might save. . . . . .

HORSE SENSE

Janet ripped her dress. . . . .

JANITOR

Katherine accomplished it. . . . .

KATYDID

To spear many times. . . . .

LANCELOT

Bank lending to a few people. . . . . . .

LONESOME

Magician's Springtime show. . . . .

MATRIX

Why a psychotic does something. . .

LOCOMOTIVE

A 2,000 pound gravesite. . . . .

KRYPTON

Forgot what I need at the market. . . . .
LISTLESS

Accurate current events. . . . .
NEWSREEL

Forbidding one to stay inside. . . . .
OUTLAW

Two lovers strolling. . . . .
MEANDER

Only the truth. . . . .
NOBLE

A not-new family room. . . . .
OLDEN

Twin physicians. . . . .
PARADOX

Speeding by you. . . . .
PASTEURIZE

Someone else is smart. . . . .

OTHERWISE

Where you are after she pushes you away. .

OFFER

Helping out with agricultural duties. .

PHARMACIST

How a hog might describe himself. . . . . . .

PYGMY

Following the game's rules. . . . .

PLAYWRIGHT

A parrot who has flown away. . . . .

POLYGON

Four times value of Russian money. .

QUADRUPLE

Bunking down in the street. . . . .

ROADBED

Hurrying and scurrying. . . . .
RUSSIAN

What those in trouble cry out. . . . .
POROUS

Beacon guiding planes in storms. . . . .

PILOT LIGHT

Rubber doo-doo. . . . .
SHAMPOO

The Queen does it in the restroom. . .

ROYAL FLUSH

A paid athlete not yet 20 years old. . . . .
PROTEIN

Flinging a dangerous eating utensil. . .
PITCHFORK

A circular time keeper. . . . .
O'CLOCK

Mending a fishing implement. . . . .
NETWORK

An Englishman misses his "elevenses". . .
NAUGHTY

A man consumed this much beef? . . . . .
MEDIATE

When you're blindfolded. . . . .
NAZI

Dog and the fruit he loves. . . . .
MELANCHOLY

Catching 40 winks with your cousin. . . . . .
NAPKIN

More than "e". . . . .
OVARY

How do you make a sweater?. . . . .
UNIT

Words on a bathroom floor. . . . .
TEXTILE

Pitched in the garbage. . . . .
THROUGHOUT

Place adhesive all over a woman. . . . .
TAPER

One who sums up all the "t"s. . . . . . .
TEETOTALER

Flakey footwear. . . . .
SNOWSHOES

Hairdressers do this to some women. . .
STREAKER

A young boy from Warsaw. . . . .
TADPOLE

When a Broadway play fails. . . . . . .
SHOWDOWN

Cancelled TV series. . . . .
SHOW OFF

True report from private to captain. . . .
SURREAL

Foursome waiting their turn at golf. . .
TEA PARTY

To rule, to govern. . . . .
TERRAIN

To inform a girl, give her information. . . . . .
TELLER

Money you pay for being naughty. . . . . . .
SYNTAX

On prehistoric hunter to another. . . . .
SPIRIT

A woman who cleans for a clothier. .
TAILOR-MADE

Taking care of a girl. . . . .
TENDER

Having a few rubber wheels. . . . .
TIRESOME

Why did the train derail?. . . . .
TRACTOR

A drink made from a very tall plant. . . . .
TREATY

This happens when you cry. . . . .
TYRANNIZE

When a cop carries his gun high. . . . .
UPHOLSTER

Okay, you know the secret password. . . . .
URINE

A disease afflicting magicians. . . . . .
TRICHINOSIS

Where a female seducer will burn. . . . . . .

VAMPIRE

The tattered end of a rope. . . . .

WEEKEND

What skiers would advise for warmth...

WEAR DOWN

A post card that sings. . . . .

VOICE MAIL

When looking for a dwelling, ask this.

WAREHOUSE

Sign of a happy dog. . . . .

WAGON

Skiers' advice for keeping warm. . . . . .

WEAR DOWN

Place where all promises are kept. . . . . . .

VOWEL

Formal dance moving back and forth. .
VOLLEYBALL

Water to sit in until others come. . .
WADING POOL

Unnecessary words spoken on stage. .
WAISTLINE

Creature living in deep reservoir. . . . .
WELLBEING

A smart piece of land. . . . .
WISEACRE

A 36" appendage. . . . .
YARDARM

A fish caught and taken away. . . . .
UNSCHOOLED

Say to a stranger at the door. . . . .
YOO HOO

Tell sadness to leave. . . . .

WOEBEGONE

What to do with a large bell. . . . .

RINGER

Biggest breast supporter. . . . .

ZEBRA

Male greeting, in the 'hood. . . . .

YOEMAN

It just isn't possible to have a civil war.

If it's tourist season, we should be able to shoot them.

I was on an elevator the other day and the operator kept calling me "Son." When I asked him why, he said, "I brought you up, didn't I?"

Did you ever notice that when you put the two words "the" and "IRS" together, it spells "theirs."

Washington State just legalized gay marriage and the use of marijuana.
This makes perfect Biblical sense because *Leviticus 20:13* says, "If a man lie with another man they should be stoned."
We just hadn't interpreted it this way before.

Woody Allen said it: "I discovered a new oral contraceptive last night. I asked a girl out and she said no."

One nice thing about narcissists: they don't talk about other people.

Middle age is when you stop growing at both ends and begin growing in the middle.

I lost my mind, and I'm sure the kids took it.

I think the freezer deserves a light, too.

I didn't want to believe my father was stealing from his job as a road worker. But when I got home, all the signs were there.

What did the blanket say when it fell off the bed? Oh sheet!

THINGS MY PARENTS TAUGHT ME

They taught me irony: "Keep crying like that and I'll give you something to cry about."

They taught me foresight: "Be sure your underwear is clean, in case you're hit by a bus."

They taught me religion: "You'd better pray this comes out of the carpet!"

They taught me stamina: "You'll sit there until every single pea is gone from your plate."

They taught me about hypocrisy: "For the hundredth time, stop exaggerating."

They taught me anticipation: "You just wait 'til we get home!"

They taught me logic: "Because I said so, that's why!"

My parents taught me genetics: "You're just like your mother/father!"

My parents taught me medical science: "If you don't stop making that face, it'll freeze that way."

My parents taught me wisdom: "When you're as old as I am, then you'll understand."

My father taught me about the circle of life: "I brought you into this world and I can take you out."

My mother taught me genetics: You're just like your father."

My mother taught me ESP: "Put your sweater on, don't you think I know when you are cold?"

My mother taught me behavior modification: "Stop acting like your father."

My mother taught me humor: "When the lawn mower cuts off your toes, don't come running to me!"

YOU KNOW YOU'RE IN A REDNECK CHURCH

If opening day of deer season is recognized as an official church holiday

If the finance Committee refuses to provide funds for the purchase of a chandelier because none of the members know how to play one.

If people   think "rapture" is what you get when you lift something too heavy.

If people ask when they learn Jesus fed the 5,000, whether the two fish were bass or catfish and what bait was used to catch 'em.

When the pastor says, "I'd like to ask Bubba to help take up the offering" and five guys and two women stand up.

If the choir is known as the 'OK Chorale"

If "thou shalt not covet" applies to huntin' dogs too.

If a member of the church requests to be buried in his 4-wheel drive truck because, "It ain't never been in a hole it couldn't get out of."

If in a congregation of 500 members, there are only seven last names in the church directory.

If the baptismal pool is a #2 galvanized "wheeling" washtub.

If the choir robes were donated by, and embroidered with, the logo from "Billy Bob's Barbecue"

If the collection plates are really hub caps from a '56 Chevy.

If instead of a bell you are called to service by a duck call.

If the minister and his wife drive matching pickup trucks.

WORD PLAY, SEX DIVISION

Chess players check their mates.

Carpet layers do it on the floor.

Carpenters hammer it harder.

Clock makers do it mechanically.

Clowns do it for laughs.

Bookkeepers do it with double entry.

Bricklayers lay all day.

Chemists like to experiment.

Bicyclists do it in ten speeds.

Barbers do it with shear pleasure.

Cheerleaders do it with enthusiasm.

Basketball players score more often.

Bosses delegate the tasks to others.

Doctors do it with patients.

Engineers charge by the hour.

Divers do it deeper.

Cowgirls do it bareback.

Executives have large staffs.

Detectives do it under cover.

Drummers do it in 4/4 time.

Direct mailers get it in the sack.

Credit managers always collect.

Dancers do it in leaps and bounds.

Coaches whistle while they work.

Dentists do it until it hurts.

Cocktail waitresses serve highballs.

Computer gamers just can't stop.

Firemen are always hot.

Hunters do it with a bang.

Joggers do it on the run.

Lawyers do it in their briefs.

Inventors discover new positions.

Equestrians stay in the saddle longer.

Janitors clean up afterwards.

Golfers do it in 18 holes.

Handymen like good screws.

Gymnasts mount and dismount well.

Interior decorators do it all over the house.

Fishermen are proud of their rods.

Jewelers mount real gems.

Pilots keep it up longer.

Plumbers do it under the sink.

Nurses call the shots.

Painters do it in longer strokes.

Movie stars do it on film.

Musicians do it in rhythm.

Missile men have better thrust.

Models do it in any position.

Miners sink deeper shafts.

Milkmen deliver twice a week.

Divers have no problem going down under.

Magicians are quicker than the eye.

Ministers do it on Sunday.

Long distance runners last longer.

Locksmiths can get into anything.

Secretaries do it 9-5.

Salesmen have a way with their tongues.

Roofers do it on top.

Reporters do it daily.

Printers do it without wrinkling the sheets.

Racers like to come in first.

Sportscasters like an instant replay.

Mailmen come slower.

Professors do it by the book.

Writers do it in novel ways.

Wrestlers know the best holds.

Waitresses serve it piping hot.

Welders always have hot rods.

Truckers pack bigger loads.

Typists do it in triplicate.

Taxi drivers do it all over town.

Taxidermists mount everything.

Tailors make it fit.

Zoologists do it with animal instinct.

Real estate agents know all the prime spots.

Librarians do it quietly.

Students use their heads.

Policemen like big busts.

HILARIOUS ONE LINERS

JUST KIDS AT HEART

OH THE THING KIDS SAY

On being told to behave, the two-year-old said: "I'm being haive."

On being told to "come on," that same two-year-old said, "I'm come-on'ing."

A seven-year-old says, "I'm NOT an oxymoron!"

Twelve-year-old to her father, who suggested she use some elbow grease on the dishes. "Well, Mom said all I had to use was the sponge and the dish detergent."

Upon being refused a toy that was too expensive, the 3-year-old demands, "Why don't you go get some expensive money?"

A 6-year-old watches his Dad tap the walls to find the support beams to hang pictures. "Daddy, there's no one in there."

Told to make up her mind, little girl asks, "How do you put makeup on your mind?"

3-year-old after being told her shoes were on the wrong feet: "Don't be silly, Mommy. I know they're my feet."

Overheard at the pediatrician: "You said it would be a shot but it was a needle!"

Small child has dumped out the entire box of animal crackers and is examining each one. Her explanation: "It says don't eat if the seal's broken, so I'm looking for the seal."

4-year-old explains how her father knew the gender of their new kittens. "Daddy picked them up and looked underneath. I think it's printed on the bottom."

The Lord's Prayer, according to a four-year-old: "And lead us not into temptation but deliver us some email..."

A seven-year-old, scolded for peeking at the Christmas present closet, protested, "I didn't look very much! I've only got little eyes!"

"How will that help?" asked the new Kindergartener, upon being told to hold up two fingers if he had to go to the bathroom.

7 year old Asher to his 3-year-old brother: "Tell me when you fall asleep, okay?"

A little girl was diligently pounding away at her grandfather's computer. She told him she was writing a story. "What's it about?" he asked. "I don't know," she said. "I can't read."

ANSWERS TO A RECENT GED TEST

Q. Name the four Seasons.
A. Salt, Pepper, Mustard and vinegar

Q. How is dew formed?
A. The sun shines down on the leaves and makes them perspire.

Q. What guarantee will a mortgage company insist on?
A. If you are buying a house, they will insist that you are well endowed.

Q. In a Democratic Society, how important are elections?
A. Very important. Sex can only happen when a man gets an election.

Q. What happens to your body as you age?
A. When you get old, so do your bowels and you get intercontinental.

Q. What happens to a boy when he reaches puberty?
A. He says Goodbye to boyhood and looks forward to adultery.

Q. How can you delay milk turning sour?
A. Keep it in the cow.

My young grandson called last week to wish me a happy birthday. He asked me how old I am and I told him: "Sixty-two."
After a pause, he said, "Did you start at one?"

Four-year-old Susie was drinking orange juice when she got the hiccups.
"Don't give me this juice again," she said. "It makes my teeth cough."

Four-year-old girl: "Daddy, you mean you're a boy already?"

I totally take back all those times I fought having a nap when I was younger.

Second-grade city schoolteacher took her class to a farm. When they returned to school, she asked: "Okay, children, what sounds did we hear on our trip to the farm today?
"Mooooo!"
"Baaaaa!"
"Quack! Quack!"
"Get off that fuckin' tractor!"

Melanie, age five, asked her Granny how old she was. Her grandmother said she was so old, she had forgotten her age.
"Well, then, Granny you have to look at the back of your underpants. Mine says five to six."

Four-year-old Niki to an elderly, very wrinkled woman: "Why doesn't your skin fit your face?"

My nine-year-old daughter walked in while I was getting ready for work.
"What are you doing," she asked?
"Putting on my wrinkle cream, I answered.
"Oh," she said, walking away. "I thought that they were natural."

Joel, age 3, hugged and kissed his mother goodnight, and said, "I love you so much, Mommy, that when you die, I'm going to bury you under my bedroom window."

Five-year-old Pam had an earache. She knew where to find the painkiller but couldn't open the bottle. She brought the bottle to her mother, who explained that it was a childproof bottle that only adults could open. Eyes wide with wonder, Pam said, "but how does it know it's ME?"

A gay child was always getting beaten up in school. His father told him the next time it happened, to punch the bully in the nose. "I would have," said the boy, "but he's so cute."

Jack, age 3, was watching as his mother nursed his new baby sister. After a while, he said, "Mommy, why do you have two? Is one for hot and one for cold milk?"

The children were lined up for lunch in the cafeteria of a Catholic elementary school. At the near end of the table was a bowl of beautiful red apples, with a note stuck in it. "Take only ONE," the note said. "God is watching." At the far end of the table, past the meat loaf, the potato, and the green beans, was a large plate heaped with chocolate chip cookies. A child had written a note: "Take all the cookies you want. God is watching the apples."

James, age four, was listening to a Bible story. His Dad read, "The man named Lot was warned to take his wife and flee from the city, without looking back. But his wife couldn't resist. She looked back and was turned into salt."
Concerned, the little boy asked, "What happened to the flea?"

Two young boys walked into a pharmacy, picked up a box of tampons and began to the checkout.
"Son, how old are you?"
"Eight," he said.
"Do you know what these are used for?"
"Not exactly. But they're not for me, they for my brother. He's four."
"And why would he need them?"
"On TV, it says that if you use these, you can swim, play tennis, and ride a bike. Right now, he can't do none of those."

Little boy to Santa: "Dear Santa. I've been good all year. Most of the time. Once in a while. Never mind, I'll buy my own stuff."

One kid to another at the town pool: "How does that rope stop the deep water from getting into the shallow water?"

Boy: Can I go to the bathroom?
Teacher: Only if you can say the alphabet.
Boy: Okay.
ABCDEGHIJKLMNO...QRSTUVWXYZ
Teacher: Where's the P?
Boy: Halfway down my leg.

The mother of a three-year-old was startled to hear him say, "Yes, sir," to her. She explained that 'sir' was for men and 'ma'am' for women.
"So, what would you say to Daddy?"
"Yes, sir."
"Very good. And to Mama?"
"Yes, ma'am."
"And to Nana?"
He lit up and said, "Can I have a cookie?"

Six-year-old Angie returns home from school and tells her mother they had their first family planning lesson that day.
Wondering what that could be about, her mother asks, "How did it go?"
"I was so ashamed!" says the little girl.
"Sam from over the road says that the stork brings babies. Sally next door said you can buy babies at the orphanage. Peter says his little sister was bought at the hospital."
Laughing a bit, her mother says, "But that's no reason to be ashamed!"
"No, but I can't tell them that we're so poor that you and Daddy had to make me yourselves!"

A schoolteacher asked her class to construct sentences with the words defeat, detail, and defense. One pupil raised his hand and said he could make a sentence with all of them: "The cow jumped over defense and detail went over defeat."

A four-year-old stepped down from the scale, and asked: "How much do I cost?"

SAD: the moment when you realize the swing set will break if you try to use it. Your childhood is over.

It's that Moms ask if we think they are made of money. Isn't that what MOM stands for? M – made   O – of   M – money.

Learn from your parents' mistakes. Use birth control.

We are born naked, wet, and hungry. Then things get worse.

We have enough youth. How about a Fountain of Smart?

I was drying my son's hair and he was saying, "Stop! Stop!"
When I kept on drying his hair, he said, "What are you? Ear blind?"

A teacher gives her second graders a lesson on the magnet and what it does. The next day, in a written test, she includes the question, "My full name has six letters. The first one is M. I am strong and attractive. I pick up things. What am I?"
When the test papers are turned in, almost half of the students answered the question with the word "Mother."

Attending a wedding for the first time, a little girl whispers to her mother, "Why is the bride all dressed in white?"
"Because that is the color of happiness," explained the mother. "And today is the happiest day of her life!"
The child thought about this for a moment. "So why is the groom wearing black?"

Little Timmy's kindergarten class was on a field trip to their local police station where the saw pictures tacked to a bulletin board of the 10 most wanted criminals. One of the youngsters pointed to a picture and asked if it really was the photo of a wanted person. "Yes," said the policeman. "The detectives want to catch him very much." Little Timmy then asked, "Why didn't you keep him when you took his picture?"

A five-year-old is asked what he got for Christmas.
"Presents," he says.
What kind of presents?
Giving the adult an are-you-stupid look, he answers: "Christmas presents."

After the bath one evening: "My butt crack is broken. Mommy, you washed away my protective layer of dirt!"

Four-year-old Cassie said the reason the Christmas tree had a skirt was so you couldn't see its panties.

Upon seeing a vinyl record, Gary says, "That's the biggest CD I ever saw."

A little girl was talking to her teacher about whales. The teacher said it was impossible for a whale to swallow a person because its throat was too small. The little girl was confused, since in the Bible, Jonah is swallowed by a whale. Irritated, the teacher repeated that it was physically impossible for a whale to swallow a person. The little girl said, "When I get to Heaven I will ask Jonah." The teacher asked, "Well, what if you go to Hell?" The little girl replied, "Well, then you ask him."

Last night I asked my three-year-old for the iPad so I could look at my pancake recipe. She told me that Daddy was smarter because he didn't need the computer to make pancakes. Well, he uses the batter in a bottle and I make them from scratch!

A Sunday school teacher was teaching the 10 commandments to her students. After explaining the idea of "Honor thy father and mother," the teacher asked if there was a commandment teaching how to treat one's siblings. From the back, a little boy answered "Thou shalt not kill."

Two little boys, Jimmy and Jonny, are excessively mischievous. They are always getting into trouble and causing chaos around town. One day, the boys' mother heard that the local preacher in town had been successful at disciplining difficult children, so she asked the preacher to speak with the boys. The preacher agreed, but only if he could see each boy one at a time.

The mother sent Jimmy, in the morning. The preacher, a huge man with a booming voice, sat him down and asked him, "Do you know where God is, son?"The boy's mouth dropped open but no words came out.

The preacher repeated, even more sternly, "Where is God?"

The boy made no attempt to answer.

The preacher raised his voice and shook his finger in the boy's face, bellowing, "WHERE IS GOD?"

The boy screamed and bolted from the room, ran home and hid away in a closet. When the older brother found him there, he asked what had happened. The younger brother replied in a shaky voice, "We are in BIG trouble this time. God is missing, and they think we did it."

I called home the other day and six-year-old Nick answered. He was panting a little. I said, "Hi, Nick. Wow, you sound out of breath." "No, Mommy," he said. "I have more."

A little girl asked her mother, "Can I go outside and play with the boys?" Her mother replied, "No, you may not go out and play with the boys. They are too rough." The girl thought for a moment and then asked, "If I find a smooth one, can I play with him?"

A Kindergarten teacher was observing her classroom of children while they were drawing. She would occasionally walk around to see each child's work. As she got to one little girl who was working diligently, she asked what the drawing was of. The girl replied, "I'm drawing God." The teacher paused and then said, "No one knows what God looks like." Without missing a beat, the little girl replied, "Well they will in a minute."

A little girl was being taken to Disneyland by her grandparents. The grandmother was excited for the little girl when they boarded the plane, claiming that her granddaughter had gotten the Shakespeare seat.

"Why is it the Shakespeare seat?" asked the little girl.

"You are in 2-B,"said the grandmother, "so it's the Shakespeare seat."

"Don't be silly, Grandma," said the little girl. "All the seats are Shakespeare seats."

"How is that?" asked the grandmother.

"Well," said the granddaughter, "It's either seat 2-B or not 2-B."

On school picture day, after all the children had been photographed, a teacher tried to convince her students to buy the group picture. She explained how nice it would be to say when they were grown, 'There's Jennifer, and she's a lawyer," or "That's Michael, he's a doctor." A moment later, a small voice at the back of the room said, "And there's the teacher... she's dead."

On the first day of school a child handed his teacher a note from his mother. The note read: "The opinions expressed by this child are not necessarily those of his parents."

Little Danny wanted $100 and prayed for two weeks to get it, but nothing happened. He decided to write God a letter requesting the $100. When the postal service got the letter addressed to 'God, USA,' they decided to send it to the President. The President was so impressed that he sent Danny a 5 dollar bill. Danny was indeed impressed, and sat down to write a thank you letter to God, which read:

> Dear God,
>
> Thank you very much for sending the money, but I noticed that you had it sent via Washington, D.C. and as usual, those crooks deducted $95.00.
>
> Thanks,
> Danny

KIDS TELL TALES FROM THE BIBLE

Lot's wife was a pillar of salt during the day, but a ball of fire during the night.

In the first book of the bible, Guinessis, God got tired of creating the world so he took the Sabbath off.

Adam and Eve were created from an apple tree.

Noah's wife was Joan of Ark. Noah built an ark and the animals came on in pears.

The Jews were a proud people and throughout history they had trouble with unsympathetic genitals.

Samson was a strongman who let himself be led astray by a Jezebel like Delilah.

Samson slayed the Philistine's with the axe of the apostles.

Moses led the Jews to the Red Sea where they made unleavened bread, which is bread without any ingredients.

The Egyptians were all drowned in the dessert. After, Moses went up to Mountcyanide to get the Ten Commandments.

The seventh commandment is thou shalt not admit adultery.

Moses died before he ever reached Canada then Joshua led the Hebrews in the Battle of Geritol.

The great miracle in the bible is when Joshua told his son to stand still and he obeyed him.

David was a Hebrew king who was skilled at playing the liar. He fought the Finkelsteins, a race of people who lived in Biblical times.

Solomon, one of David's sons, had 300 wives and porcupines.

When Mary heard she was the mother of Jesus, she sang the Magna Carta.

When the three wise guys from the East arrived, they found Jesus in a manager.

Jesus was born because Mary had an immaculate contraption.

St. John the blacksmith dumped water on his head.

Jesus enunciated the Golden Rule, which says do unto others before they do one to you. He also explained that man doth not live by sweat alone.

The Epistles were the wives of the Apostles.

The first commandment was when Eve told Adam to eat the apple.

It was a miracle when Jesus rose from the dead and managed to get the tombstone off the entrance.

The people who followed the Lord were called the 12 decibels.

One of the Oppossums was St. Matthew who was also a taximan.

St. Paul cavorted to Christianity. He preached holy acrimony, which is another name for marriage.

Christians have only one spouse. This is called monotony.

At a Sunday school class, a teacher asked,
"What was the name of Jesus' mother?"
A girl answered, "Mary."
The teacher then asked, "And who knows
the name of Jesus' father?"
The same girl, without hesitation, answered:
"Verge."
"Verge?" The teacher was confused.
"Excuse me, but where did you get that?"
Said the girl: "Well, they're always talking
about Verge 'n' Mary..."

A father was approached by his son after
Sunday school, who said,
"I know what the Bible means!"
The father smiled and replied, "Son, you
can't know what it all 'means'!"
The son replied, "I do know!"
"Okay," said the father. "What does the
Bible mean?"
"Easy, Daddy," the young boy replied. "It
stands for Basic Information Before Leaving
Earth."

A four-year-old reciting the Lord's Prayer:
"And lead us not into temptation, but deliver
us some email..."

Told to make up her mind, Barbara says,
"How do you put makeup on your mind?"

A four-year-old wants to know:
What if Jesus had been a girl?

A fifth-grade girl asked her mother, "How
did I get here?"
Her mother said, "God sent you."
"Did God send you and Daddy too?"
"Yes, he did."
"Grammy and Grandpa? And their parents?"
"That' right."
"So you're telling me there's been no sex in
our family for over 100 years?"

A three year old noticed his private parts
while in the bath.
"Are these my brains?" he asked.
Said his mother: "Not yet."

THINGS YOU LEARN FROM YOUR KIDS

#Always look in the oven before turning it
on.

#No matter how much jello you put in the swimming pool, you cannot walk on water.

#If you hook a dog leash over the ceiling fan, the motor is not strong enough to rotate a 42-pound boy wearing Star Wars Underwear and a Superman cape.

#When you hear the toilet flush and the words "uh-oh," it's already too late.

#Super Glue is forever.

#A turtle will not walk on a leash.

#The spin cycle on the dryer will not make worms dizzy.

#It will, however, make a cat dizzy.

#Cats throw up twice their body weight when dizzy.

QUESTION AND ANSWER

What do you call a face noodle?
An Impasta!

Why did the guy get fired from the orange juice factory?
He couldn't concentrate!

What happens when you eat yeast and shoe polish?
Every morning you will rise and shine!

What is it called when a cat wins a dog show? A Cat-Has-Trophy!

What do you get from a pampered cow?
Spoiled milk!

What do lawyers wear to court?
A lawsuit.

What gets wetter the more it dries?
A towel.

What did one pencil say to the other pencil?
You're looking sharp!

What did Bacon say to Tomato?
Lettuce get together!

Why did the picture go to jail?
Because it was framed.

What is the most hardworking part of the eye?
The pupil.

What do you get when you cross a fish and an elephant?
Swimming trunks.

Where do bees go to the bathroom?
The BP station!

Who earns a living driving their customers away?
A taxi driver!

How do you shoot a killer bee?
With a bee-bee gun.

How do you drown a hipster?
In the mainstream.

How do you make Holy Water?
Boil the Hell out of it.

What happened to the dog that swallowed a firefly?
It barked with de-light!

What did the pirate say on his 80th birthday?
Aye matey!

What stays in the corner and travels all over the world? A stamp.

Why did the computer go to the doctor?
Because it had a virus.

Why are frogs so happy?
They eat whatever bugs them.

What do you get when you cross a cow and a duck? Milk and quackers!

What do you call a sleeping bull?
A bulldozer.

What is the tallest building in the world?
The library. It has the most stories!

What do you call a belt with a watch on it?
A waist of time.

Why is England the wettest country?
Because the queen has reigned there for years.

What do get when you cross a vampire and a snowman? Frostbite.

What is the best day to go to the beach?
Sunday, of course!

What bow can't be tied?
A rainbow.

What season is it when you are on a trampoline?
Spring time.

Where did the computer go to dance?
To a disc-o.

What has one head, one foot and four legs?
A bed.

What is the difference between a school-teacher and train?
A teacher says spit out your gum and a train says "chew-chew-chew!"

Why did the birdie go to the hospital?
To get a tweetment.

What do you call someone who is afraid of Santa?
A Clause-traphobic.

What sound do porcupines make when they kiss? Ouch!

Why was the guy looking for food on his friend?
Because he said "Dinner is on me!"

Did you hear the joke about the roof?
Never mind, it's over your head.

What is brown and has a head and a tail but no legs?
A penny!

Why didn't the skeleton go to the dance?
Because he had no-body to go with.

How do crazy people go through the forest?
They take the psycho path.

What do prisoners use to call each other?
Cell phones.

What goes through towns, up and over hills but doesn't move? The road!

Why was there thunder and lightning in the lab? The scientists were brainstorming!

Why did Tony go out with a prune?
Because he couldn't find a date.

What do you call a funny mountain?
Hill-arious.

What did the candle say to the other candle? I'm going out tonight.

Why couldn't the pirate play cards?
Because he was sitting on the deck!

What did the janitor say when he jumped out of a closet? SUPPLIES!

Why did the traffic light turn red?
You would too if you had to change in the middle of the street!

What never asks questions but receives a lot of answers? The telephone.

How do you make an octopus laugh?
With ten-tickles.

Why can't your nose be twelve inches long?
Because then it would be a foot!

What has four wheels and flies?
The garbage truck!

What starts with a P, ends with an E and has a million letters in it?
A post office!

Why should you take a pencil to bed?
To draw the curtain!

How many books can you put in an empty backpack?
One! After that it's not empty!

Why did the robber take a bath?
Because he wanted to make a clean getaway.

Why did the boy tiptoe past the medicine cabinet?
He didn't want to wake the sleeping pills!

What do you get when you cross a fridge with a radio? Cool Music.

What goes up when the rain comes down? An umbrella.

Why did the belt go to jail?
Because it held up a pair of pants!

What did the stamp say to the envelope?
Stick with me and we will go places!

What kind of lights did Noah use on the Ark?
Flood lights!

Why don't you see giraffes in elementary school? Because they're all in High School!

Which month do soldiers hate the most?
The month of March!

What did the painter say to the wall?
One more crack like that and I'll plaster you!

Why do golfers wear two pairs of pants?
In case they get a hole in one!

Why did Goofy put a clock under his desk?
Because he wanted to work overtime!

Why did the boy throw the clock out the window?
Because he wanted to see time fly!

When do you stop at the green and go to the red?
While you're eating a watermelon.

Why is basketball such a messy sport?
Because you dribble on the floor!

How do you communicate with a fish?
Drop him a line!

What do sharks eat with peanut butter?
Jellyfish!

What do cats eat for breakfast?
Mice Crispies!

Why can't a leopard hide?
Because he's always spotted.

What do you give a dog with a fever?
Mustard... it's the best thing for a hot dog!

What do you get when you cross a cat with a lemon?
A sour puss!

Why do birds fly south for the winter?
It's easier than walking!

What kind of key opens a banana?
A monkey!

Why does a hummingbird hum?
It doesn't know the words!

How do you know that carrots are good for your eyesight?
Well, I've never met a rabbit wearing glasses!

Why are some fish at the bottom of the ocean?
Because they dropped out of school!

What goes up and down but doesn't move?
The temperature!

What do you get when you plant kisses?
Two-lips!

What happened to the wooden car with
wooden wheels and a wooden engine?
It wooden go!

What did one eyeball say to the other?
Between you and me, something smells.

Which weighs more, a ton of feathers or a
ton of bricks?
Neither... they both weigh a ton!

Did you hear about the party a little girl had
for her Barbie dolls? It was a Barbie-Q!

What do you call a rabbit with fleas?
Bugs Bunny!

Why did the girl bring lipstick and eye
shadow to school?
She had a make-up exam!

What is a bubble's favorite drink?
Soda POP!

What do bulls do when they go shopping?
They CHARGE!

What stays on the ground but never gets dirty?
Shadows.

Name a city where no one goes.
Electricity!

What's the difference between a cat and a frog? A cat has nine lives but a frog croaks every night!

I can run but not walk, have a mouth but can't talk, and a bed but don't sleep. What am I?
A river!

What runs but can't walk?
The faucet!

When is the best time to go to the dentist?
Tooth-hurty!

What kind of bed does a mermaid sleep in?
A water bed!

What kind of crackers do firemen like?
Firecrackers!

What word looks the same backwards and
upside-down? 'Swims.'

Why did the barber win the race?
Because he took a short cut.

What's taken before you get it?
A picture!

Where does a tree store his stuff?
In the trunk!

What did the nose say to the finger?
Stop picking on me!

What did the tie say to the hat?
You go on ahead and I'll hang around!

Where do pencils go on vacation?
Pencil-vania!

Did you hear about the race between the lettuce and the tomato?
The lettuce was a "head" and the tomato was trying to "ketchup!"

What did the leopard say after he had eaten his owner? Man, that really hit the "spot"!

I'm so bright my mother calls me sun.

I heard a story about a broken pencil. I'd tell you, but it's pointless.

I broke a finger today, but on the other hand I am completely fine.

Change is hard. Have you ever tried to bend a coin?

A butcher goes on a date and says, "It was nice meating you!"

I can't believe I got fired from the calendar factory. All I did was take a day off!

I wonder if Earth makes fun of other planets for having no life.

It's been scientifically proven that having too many birthdays can kill you!

Silence is golden. Duct tape is silver.

I would hate to work as an origami teacher. Too much paperwork.

It was the end of the day when I parked my police van in front of the station. As I gathered my equipment, my K-9 partner Harry, was barking, and I saw a little kid staring in at me
"Is that a dog you got there?" he asked.
"It sure is I replied.'
Puzzled, the kid looked at me, and then towards the back of the van. Finally, he said, "What did he do?"

A little girl was watching her parents dress for a party. When she saw her father donning his tuxedo, she warned,
"Daddy, you shouldn't wear that suit!"
And why not, darling?"
"You know that it always gives you a headache the next morning."

While walking in front of the church, the minister heard the intoning of a prayer that nearly made his collar wilt. Apparently, his seven year old son and his playmates had found a dead bird. They had a small box and cotton batting and dug a hole to make ready for the disposal of the deceased. The minister's son was chosen to say the appropriate prayers and with dignity intoned his version of what he thought his father always said: "Glory be unto the Father and unto the Son, and into the hole he goes!"

A little boy was looking through the pages of an old family bible. Suddenly, something fell out of the bible. He picked it up, and what he saw was an old leaf that had been pressed in between the pages. "Mom, look what I found!" the boy called out.
"What have you got there dear?"
With astonishment in the young boy's voice, he answered, "I think its Adam's underwear!"

A young boy said "I'm glad I'm only six, this is the oldest I've ever been in my whole life."

A little girl asked her Mom,
"Mom, can I take the dog for a walk around the block?"
Mom replied, "No, because she is in heat."
"I don't understand. What does that mean?" asked the child.
"Go ask your Father, I think he's in the garage."
The little girl went outside and ran towards the garage and asks,
"Dad, may I take Skippy for a walk around the block? I asked Mom, and she said the dog was in heat and to ask you what that means."
Dad said, "Bring Skippy over here." The father soaked a rag with gasoline and dabbed the dog's backside to disguise the scent and said, "You can go now, but keep Skippy on the leash, and only one time around the block."
The little girl left and returned a few minutes later with no dog on the leash.
Surprised, Dad asked, "Where's Skippy?"
The child said, "She ran out of gas half way down the block, and another dog is pushing her home."

A Sunday school teacher began her lesson with a question.
"Children", what do we know about God?"
A hand shot up in the air.
"He is an artist!" said the little boy.
"Really, how do you know?" the teacher asked.
"You know, Our Father who does art in Heaven."

For his birthday, little Johnny asked for a 10 speed bike. His father said, "Son, we'd give you one, but the mortgage on this house is $300,000, and your mother just lost her job. There's no way we can afford it."
The next day, the father saw Johnny heading out the front door with a suitcase.
So he asked, "Son, where are you going?'
The boy told him, "I was walking past your bedroom last night and heard you telling Mom that you were pulling out. Then, I heard her telling you she was coming too."
And I'm not staying here alone with no bike and a $300,000 mortgage"

While working for an organization that delivers lunches to the elderly, I took my four-year-old daughter with me one day. She was staring at a pair of false teeth soaking in a glass. She turned and whispered to me. "The tooth fairy will never believe this!"

A little girl had just finished her first day of school. "I'm just wasting my time," she said to her mother. "I can't read, I can't write, and they won't let me talk!"

HILAROUS ONE LINERS

QUESTIONS & ANSWERS

Q: What is your date of birth?
A: July 15th.
Q: What year?
A: Every year.

Q: How old is your son, the one living with you?
A: Thirty-eight or thirty-five, I can't remember which?
Q: How long has he lived with you?
A: Forty-five years.

Q: What do you call a man who just lost his brain?
A: Divorced.

Q: Which spice is the worst at keeping secrets?
A: Thyme.

Q: How many programmers does it take to change a light?
A: None. That's a hardware issue.

Q: How does Bill Gates enter his house?
A: He uses Windows.

Q: If pro is the opposite of con, what is the opposite of progress?
A: Congress!

Q: Why can't a bicycle stand alone?
A: It's two tired.

Q: What do you call a woman who sets her bills on fire?
A: Bernadette.

Q: Why do bakers work early hours?
A: Because they knead dough.

Q: Why couldn't the pony speak?
A: Because he was a little horse.

Q: What rock group has four men who can't sing?
A: Mount Rushmore.

Q: What was the shy rock's wish?
A: To be a little boulder!

Q: What did the Pacific Ocean say to the Atlantic Ocean?
A: Nothing, it just waved.

Q: What do you get when you cross a dog with a telephone?
A: A golden receiver.

We're going to Seattle. Who's "Attle?"

Ever wonder why there's a stairway to heaven, but a highway to hell?
There's apparently more traffic going to hell.

Johnny's mother had three children. The first child was named April, the second child was named May? What was the third child's name? Johnny, of course. Try to pay attention.

There is a clerk at the butcher shop. He's five feet ten inches tall and wears size 13 sneakers. What does he weigh? Meat. He's a butcher and he weighs meat.

How much dirt is there in a hole that is two feet by three feet by four feet?
There is no dirt in a hole.

What word in the English language is always spelled incorrectly? 'Incorrectly,' of course!

Bill was born on December 28th, yet his birthday is always in the summer. How come? Bill lives in the Southern Hemisphere.

Dear Paranoid People who check behind their shower curtains for murderers... If you do find one, what's your plan?

You know that tingly feeling you get when you really like somebody?
That's common sense leaving your body.

If love is the answer, could you please rephrase the question?

-Lily Tomlin

If a leper gives you the finger, do you have to give it back?

Have you got bills to pay? Please give it back! He looks so silly, bald!

You know that look women get when they want sex? No? Well, neither do I.

If the good die young, what does that say about senior citizens?

What did the alien dandelion say to the earth dandelion? "Take me to your weeder."

"Children, what comes after O?"
"Yeah!"

"Waiter, do you have frog's legs?"
"No, sir, I've always walked like this."

THE UNANSWERABLE QUESTIONS

Why do we find it necessary to nail down the lid of a coffin?

Why do you need a driver's license to buy liquor if you can't drink and drive?

Why isn't there a special name for the tops of your feet?

Why is a boxing ring really square?

Why is the third hand on a watch called the second hand?

Why have we never seen the headline: "Psychic Wins Lottery?"

Can fat people go skinny-dipping?

Why is lemon juice made with artificial flavor, while dishwashing liquid is made with real lemons?

How important does a person have to be before they are considered assassinated instead of murdered?

Once you're in heaven, do you get stuck wearing the clothes you were buried in for all eternity?

How is it that we put man on the moon before we figured out it would be a good idea to put wheels on luggage?

Why is it that people say they 'slept like a baby,' when babies wake up every two hours?

Why do people pay to go up tall buildings and pay money at the top to look in binoculars at things on the ground?

Why do doctors leave the room while you change? They are going to see you naked anyway...

Shouldn't they make mouse-flavored cat food?

Why is 'bra' always singular and 'panties' always plural?

Why would a Kamikaze pilot ever wear a helmet?

If corn oil is made from corn, and vegetable oil is made from vegetables, then what is baby oil made from?

Why do the Alphabet Song and 'Twinkle, Twinkle Little Star' have the same tune?

Is there ever a day that mattresses are not on sale?

Why do people constantly return to the refrigerator in hopes that something new will have materialized?

Did you ever notice that when you blow air in a dog's face, he gets mad at you, but when you take him for a ride in the car, he sticks his head out the window the whole time?

Why do we press harder on the buttons of the remote control even when we know the batteries are going dead?

Why do banks charge a fee for 'insufficient funds' when they know there isn't enough money in the account in the first place?

Why do people believe you when you say there are four billion stars, but check when you say the paint is wet?

Why would a Kamikaze pilot ever wear a helmet?

Why is 'abbreviated' such a long word?

Why do people run a vacuum cleaner over a thread a dozen times, when it would save time to simply bend down and pick it up?

Why do the plastic bags for produce at the grocery store never open from the end you try first?

Why is it that no matter what color bubble bath you use, the bubbles are always white?

How do dead bugs get into those enclosed light fixtures?

Why is it that whenever you attempt to catch something that's falling off the table, you always manage to knock something else over?

How come you never hear father-in-law jokes?

In winter, why do we try to keep the house as warm as it was in summer when we complained about the heat?

What if there were no hypothetical questions?

How come rain drops but snow falls?

If a deaf child signs swear words, does his mother wash his hands with soap?

If someone with multiple personality disorder threatens to kill himself, is it a hostage situation?

Can vegetarians eat animal crackers?

If the police arrest a mute, do they still tell him he has the right to remain silent?

Would a fly without wings be called a walk?

What should you do if you see an endangered plant being eaten by an endangered animal?

If a turtle loses its shell, is it naked or homeless?

Why do they put a braille message on drive-through bank machines?

If you try to fail and succeed, what have you done?

If you ate both pasta and antipasto, would you still be hungry?

What was the best thing before sliced bread?

Why do shops put up signs that say GUIDE DOGS ALLOWED? Dogs can't read and their owners are blind.

Do infants enjoy infancy as much as adults enjoy adultery?

Can an atheist get insurance against acts of God?

Why is there an expiration date on sour cream?

Why are the first five days after the weekend always the hardest?

Why is the third hand on a watch called the second hand?

If a word is misspelled in the dictionary, how would we ever know?

If Webster wrote the first dictionary, where did he get the words?

Why are they called "stands" when they are made for sitting?

Why do "tug boats" push their barges?

How come slow down and slow up mean the exact same thing?

Why do we say "after dark" when we mean "after light?"

Why is "phonics" not spelled the way it sounds?

If love is blind, why is lingerie so popular?

If all the world is a stage, where is the audience sitting?

How come "overlook" and "oversee" mean opposite things?

Is it a good thing is a vacuum really sucks?

Why are a wise man and a wise guy opposites?

Doesn't "expecting the unexpected" make the unexpected expected?

Why do they call it a TV set when you only have one?

Isn't it silly to sing "Take me out to the ball game" when we're already there?

We say that something is out of whack. What's a whack?

Why do we put our bath towels in the wash? Aren't we clean when we use them?

And how come glue doesn't stick to the inside of the bottle?

Ever notice? We put suits in garment bags and garments in a suitcase.

Isn't it crazy that we drive on a parkway and park in the driveway?

If we're not meant to have midnight snacks, why is there a light in the fridge?

Christmas is an odd holiday. What other time of the year do you sit in front of a dead tree and eat candy out of your socks?

Why are actors IN movies but ON television?

If a deaf person goes to court, do they still call it a hearing?

If nobody cares that Jimmy cracked corn, then why are we still singing about it?

What disease did cured ham have?

If a turtle doesn't have a shell, is he homeless or naked?

Would a fly without wings be called a walk?

Who decided that a round pizza should go in a square box?

Can you cry underwater?

Why was King George VI's first name Albert?

How do you know when it's time to tune your bagpipes?

Why aren't there any B batteries?

What if the Hokey Pokey isn't what it's all about?

How is it that one careless match can start a forest fire, but it takes a whole box to start a campfire?

How many roads must a man travel down before he admits he's lost?

How do I set my laser printer to STUN?

If practice makes perfect and nobody's perfect ... why practice?

In a country of free speech, why do we have telephone bills?

Why does the sun lighten our hair but darken our skin?

Why can't women put on mascara with their mouth closed?

Why is it that doctors call what they do a "practice?"

Why is the man who invests all your money called a broker?

Why is the time of day with the slowest traffic called rush hour?

When dog food is new and improved, who does the taste testing?

Why didn't Noah swat those two mosquitos?

You know that indestructible stuff they use to make the black box on an airplane? Why don't they make the whole plane out of that stuff?

Why are they called apartments when they are all stuck together?

Can dogs have dog days?

A French policeman stops a car and asks the gentleman is he's been drinking.
An Englishman admits he's been drinking all day, that his daughter got married that morning to a Frenchman, and that he was drinking champagne and several bottles of wine at the reception and quite a few glasses of single malt thereafter.
The policeman is shocked and proceeds to give the man a breath test for alcohol.
POLICEMAN: Monsieur, do you understand why, under French law, you are about to be arrested?
ENGLISHMAN: Officer, this is a British car. My wife is driving—on the other side.

CUSTOMER TO CUTE WAITRESS: I've been trying to get your attention but you keep avoiding me. So here I am, in the kitchen, to ask you if you'd like to have dinner with me tonight.
WAITRESS: Of course. Thank you.
CUSTOMER: Then why wouldn't you even make eye contact with me?
WAITRESS: I thought you wanted more coffee.

THIS STUDENT GOT A ZERO ON HIS EXAM. WE THINK HE SHOULD HAVE AT LEAST PASSED.

Q. In which battle did Napoleon die?
A. His last battle.

Q. Where was the Declaration of Independence signed?
A. At the bottom of the page.

Q. How can you drop a raw egg onto a concrete floor without cracking it?
A. Any way you like. Concrete floors are very hard to crack.

Q. If it took eight men ten hours to build a wall, how long would it take four men to build it?
A. No time at all. The wall is already built.

Q. How can you lift an elephant with only one hand?
A. You will never find an elephant with only one hand.

Q. If you had three apples and four oranges in one hand and four apples and three oranges in the other, what would you have?
A. Very large hands.

Q. How does one go 8 days without sleep?
A. You sleep at night.

THESE ARE ACTUAL QUESTIONS FROM AN AUSTRALIAN TOURISM WEBSITE.

Q: Which direction is North in Australia?
A: Face south and turn 180 degrees. Contact us when you get there and we'll send the rest of the directions.

Q: Can I bring cutlery into Australia?
A: Why? Just use your fingers like we do.

Q: Will I see kangaroos in the street?
A: Depends on how much you've had to drink.

Q: I want to walk from Perth to Sydney...Can I follow the railroad tracks?
A: Sure. It's only 3,000 miles. Take lots of water.

Q: Does it ever rain in Australia? I've never seen it rain on TV, so how do plants grow?
A: We import all plants fully grown, and then just sit around watching them die.

Q: Can you give me some information about hippo racing in Australia?
A: Af-ri-ca is the big triangle shaped continent south of Europe. Aus-tra-lia is that big island in the middle of the Pacific which... Oh, forget it. Hippo racing takes place every Tuesday in Brisbane. Come naked.

Q: Can I wear high heels in Australia?
A: You are a British politician, right?

Q & A, MEDICAL DIVISION

Q: Should I have a baby after 35?
A: No, 35 children is quite enough.

Q: I'm two months pregnant now. When will my baby move?
A: With any luck, right after he finishes college.

Q: What is the most reliable method to determine a baby's sex?
A: Childbirth.

Q: My wife is five months pregnant and so moody that sometimes she's borderline irrational.
A: So what's your question?

Q: My childbirth instructor says it's not pain I'll feel during labor, but pressure. Is she right?
A: Yes, in the same way that a tornado might be called an air current.

Q: Is there any reason for me to be in the delivery room while my wife is in labor?
A: Not unless the word "alimony" means anything to you.

Q: Is there anything I should avoid while recovering from childbirth?
A: Yes. You should have avoided pregnancy altogether.

HUSBAND TO WIFE: Sure, I'd love a second honeymoon...who with?

WIFE TO HUSBAND: My God! Have we been burgled?
HUSBAND TO WIFE: Nope. The grandkids came to visit while you were gone.

A man boarded a plane with six children. After they got settled in their seats, a woman sitting across the aisle leaned over to him and asked,
"Are all of those children yours?"
He replied, "No, ma'am. I work for a condom company. These are customer complaints."

HOW DO YOU KNOW YOU'RE GETTING OLD?

One: you're getting old when you don't care where your spouse goes just as long as you don't have to go along.
Two: you're getting old when you are cautioned to slow down by the doctor, not the police.
Three: you're getting old when you have a choice of two temptations and you choose the one that gets you home earlier.

QUESTIONS "DEAR ABBY" COULD NOT ANSWER

"Dear Abby, two women moved in across the hall from me. These two women go everywhere together and I've never seen them with a man. Do you think they could be Lebanese?"

"Dear Abby, You told some woman whose husband had lost interest in sex to send him to a doctor. Well, my husband has lost all interest in sex, and he is a doctor. Now what do I do?"

"Dear Abby, What can I do about all the sex, nudity, foul language and violence on my VCR?"

"Dear Abby, I am a 23-year-old liberated woman who has been on the pill for two years. It's getting expensive and I think my boyfriend should share half the cost, but I don't know him well enough to discuss money with him."

"Dear Abby, My forty-year-old son has been paying a psychiatrist fifty dollars an hour every week for two and a half years. He must be crazy."

"Dear Abby, my mother is mean and short tempered. I think she is going through mental pause."

"Dear Abby, I have a man I can't trust. He cheats so much on me, I'm not even sure the baby I'm carrying is his."

REMEMBER THE FIRST "HOLLYWOOD SQUARES"?

Answers were always off the cuff, not scripted. This spontaneous wit often had the audience laughing for ten or fifteen minutes and nobody tried to stop them.

Q: Do female frogs croak?
A: If you hold their little heads under water long enough. (Paul Lynde)

Q: If you're going to take a parachute jump, at least how high should you be?
A: Three days of steady drinking should do it. (Charley Weaver)

Q: True or false, a pea can last 5,000 years.
A: Boy, it sure seems that way sometimes. (George Gobel)

Q: Which of your five senses tends to diminish as you get older?
A: My sense of decency. (Charley Weaver)

Q: You've been having trouble getting to sleep. Are you probably a man or a woman?
A: That's what's been keeping me awake. (Don Knotts)

Q: Paul, why do Hell's Angels wear leather?
A: Because chiffon wrinkles too easily. (Paul Lynde)

Q: According to Cosmopolitan magazine, if you meet a stranger at a party and you think that he's attractive, is it okay to come out and ask him if he's married?
A: No. Wait until morning. (Rose Marie)

Q: What are "Just Do It," "I Can Help," and "I Can't Get Enough?"
A: I don't know, but it's coming from the next apartment. (George Gobel)

Q: As you grow older, do you tend to gesture more or less with your hands while talking?
A: One more growing old question, Peter, and I'll give you a gesture you'll never forget. (Rose Marie)

Q: Charlie, you've just decided to grow strawberries. Are you going to get any the 1st year?
A: Of course not. I'm too busy growing strawberries. (Charley Weaver)

Q: Can boys join the Camp Fire Girls?
A: Only after lights out. (Marty Allen)

Q: In bowling, what's a perfect score?
A: Ralph, the pin boy. (Rose Marie)

Q: When you pat a dog on its head, he will wag his tail. What will a goose do?
A: Make him bark? (Paul Lynde)

Q: During a tornado, are you safer in the bedroom or in the closet?
A: Unfortunately, Peter, I'm always safe in the bedroom. (Rose Marie.)

Q: If you were pregnant for two years, what would you give birth to?
A: Whatever it is, it would never be afraid of the dark. (Paul Lynde)

Q: Jackie Gleason recently revealed that he firmly believes in them and has actually seen them on at least two occasions. What are they?
A: His feet. (Charley Weaver)

Q: Back in the olden days, when great Grandpa put horseradish on his head, what was he trying to do?
A: Get it in his mouth. (George Gobel)

Q: According to Ann Landers, is there anything wrong with getting into the habit of kissing a lot of people?
A: It got me out of the army. (Charley Weaver)

Q: Who stays pregnant for a longer period of time, your wife or your elephant?
A: Who told you about my elephant? (Paul Lynde)

Q: According to Ann Landers, what are two things you should never do in bed?
A: Point and laugh. (Paul Lynde)

Where do you see yourself five years from now? In the mirror, as always.

The teacher asks her class, "What do you call a person who keeps on talking when people are no longer interested?"
The class responds: "A teacher!"

Did you hear the one about the Liberty Bell? Yeah, it cracked me up!

What is the most common remark made by retirees in an antique shop?
I remember that.

If you throw a cat out of a car window, does it become kitty litter?

What kind of tea did the American colonists thirst for? Liberty!

What did the buffalo say to his child when he went away on a trip?
Bison.

What is "out of bounds?"
An exhausted kangaroo.

What did one flag say to the other flag?
Nothing. It just waved.

What do you call a good looking, intelligent, sensitive man?
A rumor.

What do you call a man who makes faces all day? A clockmaker.

What's the difference between mechanical engineers and civil engineers?
Mechanical engineers build weapons, and civil engineers build targets.

Why are teddy bears never hungry?
They're stuffed.

WHY TEACHERS DRINK

Q: In a democratic society, how important are elections?
A: Very important. Sex can only happen when a male gets an election.

Q: What are steroids?
A: Things for keeping carpets on the stairs.

Q: Name a major disease from cigarettes.
A: Premature death.

Q: What is artificial insemination?
A: When the farmer does it to the bull instead of the cow.

Q: How are the main 20 parts of the body categorized (e.g. the abdomen).
A: There are 3 parts: the brainium, the borax and the abdomen. The brainium contains the brain, the borax contains the heart and lungs and the abdominal cavity contains the 5 bowels: A, E, I, O, U.

Q: What is the fibula?
A: A small lie.

Q: What does 'varicose' mean?
A: Nearby.

Q: What is the most commonly used form of birth control?
A: Most people wear a condominium.

Q: What does the term 'Ceasarean section' mean?
A: The Ceasarean section is a district in Rome.

Q: What is a seizure?
A: A Roman Emperor.

Q: What is a terminal illness?
A: When you are sick at the airport.

Q: What does the word "benign" mean?
A: Benign is what you will be after you're eight.

An ancient Greek walks into his tailor's shop with a torn pair of pants.
"Euripides?" asked the tailor?
"Yes," replied the man.

Did you hear about the elephant that was always left out and felt irrelephant?

If a man is alone in the forest with no woman to hear him is he still wrong?

Q AND A, LEGAL DIVISION

LAWYER: Now, Doctor, isn't it true that when a person dies in his sleep, he doesn't know about it until the next morning
DOCTOR: Did you actually pass the bar exam?

LAWYER: Were you present when your picture was taken?
WITNESS: Are you kidding me?

LAWYER: The youngest son, the 20-year-old, how old is he?
WITNESS: He's 20, also known as your IQ.

LAWYER: How was your first marriage ended?
WITNESS: By death.
LAWYER: Whose death?
WITNESS: Take a guess.

LAWYER: Where were you at the time of the accident?
WITNESS: I forget.
LAWYER: You forget? What else have you forgotten?

LAWYER: She had three children, correct?
WITNESS: Yes.
LAWYER: How many were boys?
WITNESS: None.
LAWYER: Were there any girls?
WITNESS: Your Honor, I think I need a new attorney.

LAWYER: Doctor, how many autopsies have you performed on dead people?
DOCTOR: All of them. The live ones put up too much of a fight.

LAWYER: Do you recall the time that you examined the body, Doctor?
DOCTOR: The autopsy was performed around 8:30 PM.
LAWYER: And Mr. Jones was dead at the time?
DOCTOR: If not, he was by the time I finished.

LAWYER: All your responses MUST be oral. Now, then, where did you go to school?
WITNESS: Oral.

LAWYER: What was the first thing your husband said to you this morning?
WITNESS: He said, "Where am I, Cathy?"
LAWYER: And why did that upset you?
WITNESS: My name is Susan.

SIGNS, LISTS, BILLBOARDS, HEADLINES, BUMPER STICKERS, NOTICES etc.

NOTICES FROM ALL OVER

After coffee break, staff should empty the pot and stand upside down on the drainboard.

Would the person who took the stepladder yesterday please bring it back; or further steps will be taken.

Automatic washing machines: please remove all your clothes when the light goes out.

Toilet out of order. Please use floor below.

HEALTH FOODS OF ALL KINDS
closed due to illness

We can repair anything. Please knock hard on the door. The bell doesn't work.

If you cannot read, this leaflet will tell you where to go to get lessons.

HEADLINES YOU CAN NEVER FORGET

Panda Mating Fails...Veterinarian Takes Over

Miners Refuse to Work After Death

Man Shoots Self Before Shooting Wife and Daughter

Police Begin Campaign to Run Down Jay Walkers

Something Went Wrong in Jet Crash, Expert Says

War Dims Hope for Peace

Cold Wave Linked to Temperatures

Juvenile Court to Try Shooting Defendant

If Strike Isn't Settled Quickly, May Last Awhile

Detroit Couple Slain; Police Suspect Homicide

Red Tape Holds Up New Bridges

Hospitals Sued by 7 Foot Doctors

Local High School Dropouts Cut in Half

Kids Make Nutritious Snacks

Astronaut Takes Blame for Gas in Spacecraft

New Study of Obesity Looks for Larger Test Group

Typhoon Rips Through Cemetery; Hundreds Found Dead

On a package of meat:
100% BEEF…made with all white meat chicken.

Thomas Edison said he had many failures, I've just found 10,000 ways that won't work.

Sign carried by man in Florida:
NOT HOMELESS
I HAVE A JOB
JUST SAYING HELLO

On a coffee cup:
I'M NOT CRAZY!
MY MOTHER HAD ME TESTED!

Tennis was originally played without racquets. You slapped the ball over the net with your bare hands. Ouch!

One has only to die to be praised.

The colonel creased a little in the middle to signify that he was bowing.

DOYLE'S DELI
Soup of the day...BEER!

Today I broke my personal record for most days lived.

SIGN IN A COMPANY CAFETERIA:
Good things come to those who work their asses off and never give up

When humans are young, we are pushed around in strollers. When we become old, we are pushed around in wheelchairs. In between, we are just pushed around.

In the vet's waiting room:
Back in 5 minutes. Sit. Stay.

SIGN ON A COMPANY NOTICE-BOARD:
This firm requires no physical fitness
program. Everyone gets enough exercise
jumping to conclusions, flying off the handle,
running down the boss, flogging dead
horses, knifing friends in the back, dodging
responsibility, and pushing their luck.

A local priest, pastor, and rabbi stood by the
side of the road holding up a sign that said,
*"The end is near! Turn yourself around now
before it's too late!"*
They planned to show the sign to each
passing car.
"Leave us alone, you religious nuts!" yelled
the first driver as he sped by.
From around the curve they heard a huge
splash. "Do you think," said one of them,
"that we should just put up a sign that says
"BRIDGE OUT AHEAD?"

On the door of a maternity floor:
PUSH. PUSH. PUSH.

In a Diner window:
We offer three kinds of service:
GOOD ... CHEAP ... FAST
You can pick any two.
GOOD service CHEAP won't be fast.
GOOD service FAST won't be cheap.
CHEAP service FAST won't be good.
Your choice.

On a fence:
Salesmen welcome. Dog food is expensive.

Outside a muffler shop: "No appointment necessary. We hear you coming."

In the window of a diner: Don't stand there and be hungry. Come on in and get fed up."

In the front yard of a funeral home: "Drive carefully. We'll wait."

On an electrician's truck: "Let us remove your shorts."

On a church billboard: "7 days without God makes one weak."

On a plumber's truck: "We repair what your husband fixed."

In a non-smoking area: "If we see smoke, we will assume you're on fire and take appropriate action."

At a GYN office: "Dr. Jones, at your cervix."

At a radiator repair shop: "Best place in town to take a leak."

Above the urinals in a golf club men's room:
Welcome to This Facility
It is the only place on the grounds
That nobody will try to change your stance
Or adjust your grip.

On the lawn of a drug rehab center:
KEEP OFF THE GRASS

ON A BILLBOARD IN CALIFORNIA: Don't join dangerous cults. Practice safe sects.

Sign along a country road:
DON'T WORRY ABOUT YOUR HEALTH.
IT'LL GO AWAY.

Ladies' room graffiti: God grant me the serenity to accept things I cannot change...the courage to change the things I can...and the weaponry to make it possible.

An actual state sign:
WELCOME TO IDAHO
ATTENTION CRIMINALS AND TERRORISTS
Over 170,000 Idaho residents have a permit to legally carry a concealed weapon.
About 60% of the rest of the population is armed but have not bothered to purchase the license, as it is not a requirement to carry a firearm. Understand, a substantial portion of the population is armed and prepared to defend themselves and others against Acts of Criminal Violence.
YOU HAVE BEEN WARNED!
However, California, New York and Illinois have disarmed their citizens for your convenience.

On the back of an Amish horse-drawn carriage:
Energy Efficient Vehicle. Runs on oats and grass. Caution: Take care.
Do not step in exhaust

On a beer billboard:
Say NO to drugs.
That way, you'll have more time to drink.

SOMEWHAT DIFFERENT DOORMATS

Nice Underwear!

THIS IS NOT A JOKE
If you ever want to see
These people again
Bring me a 5 lb rib roast
In a plain brown paper bag.
-THE DOG

GO AWAY (Come back with wine)

I will not be a doormat.
I will not be a doormat.
I will not be a doormat.
Oh, just walk all over me!

Ask not for whom
the dog barks.
It barks for thee.

BEWARE OF CAT

BEER
Gets you in the door

We love our vacuum,
We've found God,
And we gave at the office.

A Lovely Lady and a
Grumpy Old Man Live Here

COME BACK
WITH A
WARRANT

I'M REALLY GLAD
TO SEE YOU
But then, I lie like a mat.

Oh damn! Not you again!

Our dog is not a biter. He's a humper

PLEASE STAY ON THE MAT

Your visit is very important to us.
Your knock will be answered
In the order in which it was received.

You Can't Scare Us
WE HAVE A DAUGHTER

(toothbrush) I HATE MY JOB!
(toilet paper roll) OH, PLEASE!

We're the crazy neighbors
Everyone warned you about

GO AHEAD...
STEP ALL OVER ME
I'M USED TO IT

Excuse me, but the squirrel just
Told me the bird feeder's empty

T-SHIRTS SEEN AROUND TOWN

When I was a KID I wanted to be older...this
crap is not what I expected.

I could be a morning person if morning
happened at noon.

NOT ARGUING.
I'm just explaining why I'm right

NOTE TO SELF: Just because it pops into my head doesn't mean it should pop out of my mouth.

I'm having one of those days where my middle finger is answering every question

Of course I'm right! I'M BOB!

BACK OFF! I have a sister and I'm not afraid of using her!

What is this word "NO" that you speak of?

Discover Wildlife...TEACH SCHOOL!

Where the HELL are my PILLS?

Sign on a basket of fresh farm eggs: BONELESS CHICKEN 35 CENTS

Sign in a barbershop window: HAIRCUTS, ONLY $7.

Sign in the window of the barbershop down the street: WE REPAIR $7 HAIRCUTS

On a van in California:
WINEBULANCE
Stay Calm, Help is Here

The saying "God willing and the Creek don't rise" does not refer to a stream or brook. It refers to the Native American tribe called Creek and was written to the American president by a politician and diplomat who had been requested to return to Washington, D.C.

Barmaids used to keep track of customers' drinking: minding their Ps (pints) and Qs (quarts).

HEADLINES FROM ALL OVER (every one of them guaranteed to be from a real newspaper)

Cow urine makes for juicy lemons

Worker suffers leg pain after crane drops 800-pound ball on his head.

Statistics show that teen pregnancy drops off significantly after age 25.

Illiteracy an obstacle, study finds

MARIJUANA ISSUE SENT TO A JOINT COMMITTEE

Federal Agents Raid Gun Shop, Find Weapons

Homeless survive winter: Now what?

Mississippi's literacy program shows improvement.

DIANA WAS STILL ALIVE HOURS BEFORE SHE DIED.

17 REMAIN DEAD IN MORGUE SHOOTING.

Homicide victims rarely talk to police.

STUDY SHOWS FREQUENT SEX ENHANCES PREGNANCY CHANCES

City unsure why sewer smells

Bridges help people cross rivers

Bugs flying around with wings are flying bugs

CASKETS FOUND AS WORKERS DEMOLISH OLD MAUSOLEUM

Man Accused of Killing Lawyer Receives a New Attorney

Barbershop singers bring joy to school for deaf

HOSPITALS RESORT TO HIRING DOCTORS Physician Shortage Prompting Move

Man with 8 DUIs blames drinking problem

Miracle Cure Kills Fifth Patient

New sick policy requires 2-day notice

PARENTS KEEP KIDS HOME TO PROTEST SCHOOL CLOSURE

TOTAL LUNAR ECLIPSE WILL BE PROADCAST LIVE ON NORTHWOODS PUBLIC RADIO
Thanks to Ted Stein

In a Southern restaurant:
    NO WE DO NOT HAVE WI-FI
    TALK TO EACH OTHER

Starvation can lead to health hazards

Billboard: Tired of spilling beer while you drive? Our extra-wide bottle fits your cup holder!

Billboard: Where are all the news crews when we're NOT spilling something?

Fish need water, Feds say.

FOR SALE: TRUCK. Very mad mother selling 16 yr. old son's 1993 Ford Ranger. Drove 3 months before son forgot to use his brain and got caught driving drunk. $4,500 OBO. Call meanest mother in Wyoming.

Billboard outside Las Vegas:
It's only a gambling problem if you're losing.

HELPING KIDS READ GOODER. Hooked on Phonics

American Medical *Marijuana* Association.

HALLMARK CARDS: Face it. You'll never come up with anything clever on your own.

Speedo: Making us all wish we were blind.

Need a good screw? Ace Hardware

Seen by the side of the road in upstate New York: PUT THE POLITICIANS ON MINUMUM WAGE – SEE HOW FAST THINGS CHANGE!

In front of a landscaping business:
SPRING IS HERE! I'M SO EXCITED I WET MY PLANTS!

In a shop window: NOW HIRING. MUST HAVE CLUE

On a tree in the middle of deer country:
WARNING!
BAITING DEER IS ILLEGAL!
This corn pile is intended for squirrels, chipmunks and other such critters
ANY DEER FOUND EATING THIS CORN WILL BE SHOT!

(newspaper headlines)
Utah Poison Control Center reminds everyone not to take poison.

Saratoga County pays $25,000 to advertise lack of funds.

(seen posted in a ladies' room)
My boyfriend has a 30-year mortgage, a 5-year car lease and a lifetime gym membership. And he's afraid to commit.

(newspaper headlines)
Open house – Body Shapers Toning Salon! Free coffee and donuts

Trial attorney accidentally sues self.

Alzheimer's Center Prepares for An Affair to Remember

Georgia Peaches...California grown...89 cents a pound.

Hummel's—Largest Selection Ever—"If it's in stock, we have it!"

(in a pet shop): Buy a dog, get many fleas

(Billboard) We're proud of our organs!
HAMMOND

(highway sign in Vermont)
PLEASE. NEUTER YOUR PETS. And weird
friends and relatives.

NO TRESPASSING. VIOLATORS WILL BE
SHOT. SURVIVORS WILL BE SHOT AGAIN.

YES, THERE IS LIFE AFTER SUBSTANCE
ABUSE. It's just not particularly fun.

CLASSIFIED ADS NOT OFTEN SEEN

Amana washer $100. Owned by clean
bachelor who seldom washed.

Snow blower for sale. Only used on snowy
days.

Soft & genital bath tissues or facial tissue:
89 cents

'92 Toyota Hunchback - $500

Nordic Track $300 – hardly used – call Chubbie

Free puppies: part Cocker Spaniel, part sneaky neighbor's dog

Tickle Me Elmo, still in box, comes with its own 1998 Mustang, 5L, auto, excellent condition $6,800 OBO

German Shepherd. 85 lbs. Neutered. Speaks German. FREE

The Low Self-Esteem Group will meet Thursday at 7:00 PM.
Please use the back door.

PRIVATE ADVERTISEMENT. DO NOT READ.

We buy old furniture. We sell antiques.

For sale: cows, never bred. Also, gay bull.

BUMPER STICKERS

In dog years...I'M DEAD!

Forget about world peace. Visualize using your turn signal!

If you can read this, I've lost my trailer.

4 OUT OF 5 VOICES IN MY HEAD SAY GO FOR IT!

I'm a nice person, but my car is evil.

EARTH IS FULL ... GO HOME!

Life is short. Pray hard.

Love thy neighbor. Just don't get caught.

This vehicle brakes for all tag sales

My DOG is my CO-PILOT

I brake for tailgaters!!

I'M OUT OF ESTROGEN AND I HAVE A GUN

Enjoy Life. It has an expiration date

YIPPEE! I WOKE UP!

I'M SO BUSY I DON'T KNOW WHETHER I FOUND A ROPE OR LOST A HORSE.

Let me drop everything & work ON YOUR PROBLEM

I KNOW IT SOUNDS AS IF I'M IN DENIAL... BUT I'M NOT!

If it's true that we learn from our mistakes... I will soon be a GENIUS!

I'm the CRAZY AUNT everyone warned you about!

I consider ON TIME to be whenever I get there.

We'll be friends 'til we're old and senile. Then we'll be new friends.

I don't suffer from insanity, I enjoy every second of it.

Some people are alive only because it is illegal to kill them.

I used to have a handle on life, but it broke.

You're just jealous because the voices only talk to me.

I'm not a complete idiot. Some parts are missing.

To all you virgins... thanks for nothing.

Out of my mind. Back in five minutes.

God must love stupid people, because he made so many!

The gene pool could use a little chlorine.

It IS as bad as you think, and they ARE out to get you.

GOLDEN YEARS BUMPER STICKERS

I'm in the initial stages of my golden years: SS, CDs IRAs, AARP...

FLORIDA: God's Waiting Room

I'm getting so old that whenever I eat out, they ask for their money up front.

The secret of staying young is to love honestly, eat slowly, and lie about your age.

We got married for better or worse. He couldn't do any better and I couldn't do any worse.

I was always taught to respect my elders. Now I don't have anyone left to respect.

I'm not old ... I'm Chronologically Gifted!

I Brake for No Apparent Reason

I ask my wife if old men wear boxers or briefs. She said DEPENDS.

I'm so old, I no longer buy green bananas.

A CLOSED MOUTH GATHERS NO FEET

Princess, having had enough experience with Princes, seeks frog.

My mother is the travel agent for guilt trips.

If you want breakfast in bed,
Sleep in the kitchen.

SIGNS OF ALL NATIONS

Most exclusive disco in town!
Everybody welcome!

Shop sign in Abu Dahbi:
IF THE FRONT IS CLOSED PLEASE ENTER
THROUGH MY BACK SIDE.

Outside St. Petersburg:
You are welcome to visit the cemetery where
famous Russian and Soviet composers,
artists and writers are buried daily, except
Thursday.

Take notice! When this sign is under water,
the road is impassable.

Sign on an office desk in the UK:
You have a right to your opinion and I have
a right to tell you how stupid it is.

Sign on a city traffic light:
DON'T WALK. DANCE.

A hotel in Japan:
YOU ARE INVITED TO TAKE ADVANTAGE OF
THE CHAMBERMAID.

Cocktail lounge, Norway:
LADIES ARE REQUESTED NOT TO HAVE
CHILDREN IN THE BAR.

I do whatever my Rice Krispies tell me to do.

WOULD YOU LIKE TO RIDE YOUR OWN ASS?
(donkey ride in Thailand)

Graffiti in Rome: History repeats itself, but
each time the price goes up.

In the window of a taxidermy shop:
WE KNOW OUR STUFF

Hotel in Zurich:
Because of the impropriety of entertaining
guests of the opposite sex in the bedroom, it
is suggested that the lobby be used for this
purpose.

Tire shop sign: Invite us to your next blowout!

I don't like political jokes. I've seen too many of them get elected.

Seen at a car dealership in New England: Best way to get back on your feet? Miss a car payment.

Graffiti in New York City high-end clothing store:
There's a thin woman inside every fat one. I ate mine.

Sign in the front yard of a funeral home: DRIVE CAREFULLY. WE'LL WAIT.

WORK IS THE PRICE YOU PAY FOR MONEY.

On a septic tank truck: *Yesterday's Meals on Wheels.*

RESTROOM SIGNS

Be like Dad, not like sis'. Lift the lid before you piss.

Stand close. The next guy might be barefoot.

Heaven is a place where:
the police are British
the chefs Italian,
the mechanics German,
the lovers French,
and it's all organized by the Swiss.
Hell is a place where:
the police are German,,
the chefs British,
the mechanics French,
the lovers Swiss,
and it's all organized by the Italians.

FUTURE BUSINESS MERGERS

- Hale Business Systems, Mary Kay Cosmetics, Fuller Brush and W. R. Grace Company will become: Hale, Mary, Fuller, Grace.

- Polygram Records, Warner Brothers and Zesta Crackers will become: Poly, Warner, Cracker.

- 3M will merge with Goodyear and become: MMMGood.

- Zippo Manufacturing, Audi Motors, Dofasco, and Dakota Mining will merge and become: ZipAudiDoDa

- FedEx is expected to join its competitor UPS and it will become: FedUp.

- Fairchild Electronics and Honeywell Computers will become: Fairwell Honeychild.

- Grey Poupon and Docker Pants will become: Poupon Pants.

- Knotts Berry Farm and the National Organization of Women will become: Knott NOW.

- Victoria's Secret and Smith & Wesson will become: TittyTittyBangBang.

A LESSON ON BURMA SHAVE

Before interstate highways and billboard signs, the Burma Shave company advertised their product on the sides of the two-lane roads people used to get around. All over the countryside, one would find series of five small, red signs spaced 100 feet apart, each sign containing a line of a four-line couplet, and the fifth sign advertising Burma Shave, a popular shaving cream. Enjoy this little trip down memory lane!

Don't stick your elbow
Out so far
It may go home
In another car
BURMA SHAVE

Trains don't wander
All over the map
'cause nobody sits
In the engineer's lap
BURMA SHAVE

Don't lose your head
To gain a minute
You need your head
Your brains are in it.
BURMA SHAVE

Drove too long
Driver snoozing
What happened next
Is not amusing
BURMA SHAVE

Around the curve
Lickety-split
Beautiful car
Wasn't it?
BURMA SHAVE

No matter the price
No matter how new
The best safety device
In the car is you
BURMA SHAVE

A guy who drives
A car wide open
Is not thinkin'
He's just hopin'
BURMA SHAVE

Both hands on the wheel
Eyes on the road
That's the skillful
Driver's code
BURMA SHAVE

The one who drives
When he's been drinking
Depends on you
To do his thinking
BURMA SHAVE

Passing school zones
Take it slow
Let our little
Shavers grow
BURMA SHAVE

He saw the train
And tried to duck it
He kicked the gas
And then the bucket
BURMA SHAVE

A man amiss
A car a curve
He kissed the miss
And missed the curve
BURMA SHAVE

The big bad wolf
Was not let in
Because of the hair
On his chinny chin chin
BURMA SHAVE

THIS
FUNNY
OLD
LIFE

You know you're old when you fall down and wonder what else you can do while you're down there.

I'm old enough to make my own decisions...just not young enough to remember what I decided.

I've lost my mind...and I'm pretty sure the kids took it.

Age is just a number. Mine is unlisted.

You know you're getting older when there's a hole between your boobs and it's called a bellybutton.

Eat right and exercise. Die anyway.

There are only two 4-letter words that offend me...
Don't and *Stop.*
Unless, of course, they are used together.

What's the best form of birth control after fifty?
Nudity.

I'm not old. I've just been young a very long time.

My sole purpose in life is to serve as a warning to others.

One year, I decided to buy my mother-in-law a cemetery plot as a Christmas gift. The next year, I didn't buy her anything. When she asked why, I said, "Well, you still haven't used the gift I bought you last year." And then the fight started.

The guys at the barber shop asked me what actress I would like to be stuck in an elevator with. I told them the one who knows how to fix an elevator.

I'm old, tired, and pee a lot.

At my age ... Happy Hour is a nap!

Live each day like it's your last. One day you'll get it right.

I'm retired. I was tired yesterday and I'm tired again today.

The only trouble with retirement: You never get a damn day off!

I'm always somewhat disappointed when a liar's pants don't actually catch on fire.

Cat to human: I don't know how to say this, but... you don't have a hamster any more.

Young at heart ... slightly older in other places.

I don't think about dying...it's the last thing I want to do.

I don't exercise. It makes my coffee spill.

I'm speeding because I have to get there before I forget where I'm going.

Obituaries would be a lot more interesting if they told you how the person died.

I'm not old. I just need some WD-40.

Blessed are those who are cracked; for they let in light.

The aging process could be slowed down considerably if it had to work its way through Congress.

You know you're getting older when "getting lucky" means finding your car in the parking lot.

I'd rather be 60 than pregnant.

Aging seems to be the only available way to live a longer life.

How old would you be if you didn't know how old you are?

I believe in having sex on the first date. At my age, there may not be a second

WARNING: Menopause in progress ... go around the long way and do NOT make eye contact.

Husband to wife: "I wasn't yawning while you were talking. I was trying to get a word in."

ENJOY LIFE. It has an expiration date.

I finally figured out what I want to be when I get older...YOUNGER!

The heart has no wrinkles.

Grow your own dope. Plant a man!

Don't let aging get you down; it's too damn hard to get back up.

I doubt we get smarter as we get older. I think we just run out of stupid things to do.

My idea of housework is to sweep the room with a glance.

The only thing preventing me from smashing my alarm every morning is the fact that it's my phone.

A little boy asked his grandmother how old she was.
"Thirty-nine and holding," she said.
"Well, how old would you be if you let go?"

My doctor told me to start killing people.
Well, not in those exact words.
He said I had to reduce the stress in my life.
Same thing, really!

I need a six-month vacation, twice a year.

You know that awesome feeling when you get into bed, fall right asleep, stay asleep all night and wake up refreshed and ready to take on the day?
Yeah me neither!

I think more often about running away now than I did as a kid; but by the time I put my teeth in, my glasses on, and find my keys...
I forget why I'm going.

Never go to bed angry. Stay up and fight.

Sometimes, the easiest way to get your husband to do something is to suggest that he's just too old to do it anymore.

Chocolate makes your clothes shrink.

Wouldn't it be great if we could put ourselves in the dryer for ten minutes and come out wrinkle-free, back to our original shape, a couple of sizes smaller, and smelling spring-fresh!

Inside every older person is a younger person wondering what the hell happened.

Middle age is when you still believe you'll feel better in the morning.

If a woman speaks and no one is listening, the chances are her name is Mom.

Sometimes I wrestle with my inner demons and other times, we just hug and dance.

Instead of a sign that says "Do Not Disturb," I need one that says, "Already disturbed. Proceed at your own risk."

Don't take life too seriously. It's not like you're going to get out alive.

I wake up tired and go to bed wide awake!

I read recipes the same way I read science fiction. When I get to the end, I think, "Well, that's not going to happen."

A rather elderly but beautifully groomed gentleman walks into a bar. Seated there is a lovely women, probably in her 70s.
The man walks over and seats himself next to her. "So tell me, beautiful," he says, "do I come here often?"

How to Fall Down the Stairs

Step One
Step Two
Step Three Four Five
Step Ten Eleven Twelve Thirteen Fourteen
                              -Rick Spaide

Said the art dealer to the artist:
"I have good news and bad news. A gentleman was in the gallery today, asking about your work. He wondered if it would appreciate in value after your death."
"Wonderful!" replied the artist. "But what's the bad news?"
"The man is your doctor."

Elderly couple went to breakfast at a diner that advertised a Seniors' Special for $2.99. Two eggs, bacon, hash browns, and toast. "Sounds good," said the wife. "But no eggs."
"In that case, I'll have to charge you $3.49 because you're ordering ala carte," warned the waitress.
"You mean, I pay for NOT having eggs?"
"That's right."
"Okay, then, I'll have the special."
"And how would you like your eggs?"
"Raw and in the shell," said the wife.
She took those eggs home and baked a cake.

"I spent half of my money on booze, women and gambling. The other half, I wasted."
-W. C. Fields

A man has reached middle age when he is cautioned to slow down by his doctor instead of the traffic cops.

Middle age is when you have stopped growing at both ends, and have begun to grow in the middle.

When our lawn mower broke, my wife kept hinting that we should get it fixed. But somehow, I never got to it.
Meanwhile, the grass kept growing.
One day, I came home and found her sitting in the tall grass, busily snipping away with a pair of tiny sewing scissors.
I watched awhile then went into the house and came back with a toothbrush.
"When you finished cutting the grass," I said, feeling quite clever, "you might as well sweep the front walk."

The doctors say I will walk again, but I will always have a limp.

No matter how slow you go, you are still lapping everyone sitting on the couch.

A man has reached middle age when he is cautioned to slow down by his doctor instead of the traffic cops.

Got my coffee...
Got my cigarettes...
Got my computer and took my Prozak...
It's gonna be a great day!

Sometimes I pretend to be normal.
But it gets boring so I got back to being me.

A bent-over old lady hobbled into a doctor's office. She saw him only a few minutes and came out standing as straight as could be. A man in the waiting room said in amazement, "What did the doctor do to you?"
"He gave me a longer cane," she said.

By the time a man is wise enough to watch his step, he's too old to go anywhere.

You know you're getting on when you realize that caution is the only thing you care to exercise.

"Everyone should pay their taxes with a smile," says Bob.
"I tried it, but they wanted cash."

My wife was hinting about an anniversary present. She said, "I'd really like something new and shiny that goes from 0 to 150 in about three seconds."
I bought her a bathroom scale.

Don't worry about avoiding temptation. As you grow older, it will avoid you.

WIFE: These aren't wrinkles, they're laughter lines.
HUSBAND: Well, something must have been bloody hilarious.

Memories are more important than possessions...and a great deal easier to lose.

MAN: That's a really sparkling smile you have there.
WOMAN: Thanks...I put my teeth through the dishwasher this morning.

HORRIBLE THOUGHT: Hold on, if I've got a suppository in my ear...where in hell is my hearing aid?

I don't know about you, but I've thought about running away more as an adult than I ever did as a child.

There comes a time in the day that no matter the question—the answer is wine.

Banging your head against a wall uses 150 calories an hour.
Hardly seems worth it.

Women are angels. And when someone tries to break our wings, we simply continue to fly—on a broomstick, if necessary.
We're flexible like that.

HUSBAND: I'm the man or this house, so starting tomorrow, I want you to have a hot delicious meal waiting for me when I walk through the door. After dinner, while I watch NFL from my armchair, you'll bring me my slippers and a glass of cognac, and run my bath. And after I've had my bath, guess who will be combing my hair and bringing me my PJ's?
WIFE: The funeral director.

They are NOT gray hairs; they are WISDOM HIGHLIGHTS! I just happen to be extremely wise.

Always love a woman for her personality.
Every woman has, like, ten; so you can choose.

DOG: Master's home! Yay!
CAT: You're late, slave!

Well, it's finally happened.
We've become the incredibly sexy older
women that all young girls wish they
could be!

I asked my wife where she'd like to go for
our 40th anniversary.
"Some place I've never been," she said.
So I suggested the kitchen.

I quietly confided to my dear friend that I
was having an affair.
She turned to me and asked, "Are you
having it catered?"
And that, my friends, is the sad definition of
OLD.

I was talking to a girl in a bar last night.
She said to me, "If you lost a few pounds,
had a shave and got your hair cut, you'd
look great."
I said, "If I did that, I'd be talking to your
friends over there instead of you."
I came home with a black eye.

Marriage is how you get to sleep with the enemy.

We're all mature...until someone pulls out the bubble wrap.

MENOPAUSE (OTHERWISE KNOWN AS ESTROGEN ISSUES) AND HOW TO SPOT IT

Everyone around you has an attitude problem.

You're adding chocolate chips to your cheese omelet.

Your husband is suddenly agreeing to everything you say.

The dryer has shrunk every last pair of your jeans.

You're certain that everyone is scheming to drive you crazy.

Everyone seems to have just landed here from outer space.

The painkiller bottle is empty and you just bought it yesterday.

You're using your cellphone to call every bumper sticker that says, "How's my driving?"

Every person's head looks to you like an invitation to batting practice.

You haven't seen your children for weeks, although you're sure you've heard them upstairs.

I signed up for aerobics at the local gym.
They said wear loose fitting clothing.
If I had any loose fitting clothing, I wouldn't have signed up for the freaking aerobics class.

HUSBAND: The internet is so fascinating.
WIFE: That's the microwave.

My wife's intuition is so highly developed that she sometimes knows I'm wrong before I've even opened my mouth.

WIFE TO HUSBAND: For heaven's sake, Harold, you're trying to change channels with a bar of chocolate!

At my age, "getting any?" means sleep.

Dear mother-in-law,
Please don't teach me how to handle my children. I'm living with one of yours and he could use a lot of improvement.

Patient: I have a ringing in my ears.
Doctor: Don't answer!

Doctor: Mrs. Murphy, your check came back.
Mrs. Murphy: So did my arthritis.

Did you hear about the geriatric devil worshipper? He spent his life worshipping Stan.

NOTES FOR SENIOR ENTERTAINING

Who knew...

When you drink vodka over ice, it can give you kidney failure.

When you drink rum over ice, it can give you liver failure.

When you drink whiskey over ice, it can give you heart problems.

When you drink gin over ice, it can give you brain problems.

Apparently, ice is really bad for you.
Warn all your friends.

I've reached an age where any train of thought often leaves the station without me.

Watch out for the new computer virus.
It causes you to send the same email twice...
or to send a blank...
or to send that email to the wrong person...
or to send it back to the sender...
or to forget to attach the attachment ...
or to hit DELETE instead of SEND...
or worse, to hit SEND when you meant to hit DELETE.
It's called the C-NILE VIRUS and it can't be stopped!

SETTING UP A PASSWORD

WINDOWS: Please enter your password.

USER: cabbage

WINDOWS: Password must be more than 8 letters.

USER: boiled cabbage

WINDOWS: Sorry, you must include a number.

USER: 1 boiled cabbage

WINDOWS: Password can't have blank spaces.

USER: 50bloodyboiledcabbages

WINDOWS: Sorry, you must use more than one upper-case character.

USER: 50BLOODYboiledcabbages

WINDOWS: Sorry, you cannot use more than one upper-case character consecutively.

USER: 50BloodyBoiledCabbagesShovedUpYourAss IfYouDon'tGiveMeAccessNow!

WINDOWS: Sorry, no punctuation.

USER: ReallyPissedOff50BloodyCabbagesUpYourArs eIfYouDon'tGiveMeAccessNow

WINDOWS: Sorry, that password is already in use.

I don't need anger management classes. I need people to stop pissing me off!

Old age is coming at a really bad time.

Even duct tape can't fix stupid...but it can muffle the sound.

The most powerful antidepressant in the world has 4 paws and a wagging tail.

I got a job as a Wal-Mart greeter, a great find for a retiree.

I lasted less than a day.

About two hours in, my first day on the job, a very loud, decidedly unattractive (and under-dressed) woman walked into the store with her two young boys, yelling obscenities at them all the way through the entrance.

As I had been instructed, I said in a pleasant tone, "Good morning and welcome to Wal-Mart."

I then added, "Nice kids you have there. Are they twins?"

This woman stopped yelling long enough to give me a dirty look. "Don't be freaking ridiculous, dumbass! Of course they aren't twins. One is two years older than the other one and one is blond. Why the hell would you think they're twins? Are you blind or just freaking stupid?"

I replied calmly, "I'm neither blind nor stupid, Madam. I just find it hard to believe that someone actually screwed you twice. Have a good day and enjoy shopping at Wal-Mart."

My supervisor said I probably wasn't cut out for this line of work.

DOCTOR: You'll live to be 60.
PATIENT: I AM sixty.
DOCTOR: See?

I just got back from a pleasure trip. I took my sister-in-law to the airport.

If you love something, set it free. If it comes back, it will always be yours. If it doesn't come back, it wasn't yours to begin with. But if it just sits in your living room, messes up your stuff, eats your food, uses your telephone, takes your money and doesn't seem to realize that you had set it free... You either married it or gave birth to it.

Silent message from the driver's seat:
I pay attention to the signs and get in the right lane. You ignore them for miles and want me to let you in? Not going to happen.

I wonder how some people found their way out of the birth canal!

If you are always trying to be normal you will never know how amazing you can be.

–Maya Angelou

St. Peter to middle-aged man: "So you're little Bobbie, well, your dog Rex here has been going on and on about you for the last 50 years."

Blanket on ... too hot.
Blanket off ... too cold.
One leg out ... perfect!

Someday I hope to be able to afford a new iPhone...like the girl in front of me in line with the food stamps.

I stay a bit overweight because it wouldn't be fair to all the skinny people if I were attractive, intelligent, funny, AND thin.
It's a public service, really.

It's a beautiful day. I think I'll skip my meds and stir things up a bit.

266

Age is just a number. It's totally irrelevant unless, of course, you happen to be a bottle of wine.

I believe my house is haunted. Every time I look in the mirror, a crazy old lady stands in front of me so I can't see my reflection.

To err is human, to forgive, highly unlikely.

I'm on a 30 day diet. So far I've lost 15 days.

Wine is to women what duct tape is to men. It fixes everything.

Seven-year-old on the phone: "No Grandma, listen. Double-click the Internet Explorer icon."

I'm so old that I have actually dialed a rotary phone before, while listening to a Walkman, next to a black and white TV with aluminum foil on its rabbit ears!

I think too much and then put myself in a bad mood.

Dance like no one's watching. Because everyone is on their phones, so, really, no one is watching.

You know that little thing you have in your head that keeps you from saying things that you shouldn't?
Yeah, well, I don't have one of those.

If you love somebody, let them go.
If they come back, nobody wanted them.

The professor was young and it was his first class in college English. When he explained the basic part of the form of the essay, he said: "Remember, the three parts of an essay are the introduction, the body, and the confusion."

Why is patience a virtue?
Why can't "hurry the hell up" be a virtue?

At a divorce hearing a woman said, "Your Honor, I really want to divorce my husband." "Have you a reason?" asked the judge. "I have proof he is not faithful to me," she said. "Not one of our children looks anything like him!"

If you woke up breathing, congratulations, you have another chance

Imagine if women watched cooking shows the way men watch football:
WOMAN ONE: "Too much orange zest, dummy! What are you, blind?"
WOMAN TWO: "Grab the butter, you moron. NOW, or it's all over!"

There's a story in today's paper about a patient in an insane asylum who assaulted a nurse and escaped.
The headline reads:
NUT SCREWS & BOLTS

Tired Army clothes: fatigues

I wasn't planning on a run today; but the cops came out of nowhere.

My friend thinks he's smart. He said onions are the only food that can make you cry. So I threw a coconut at his head.

I hate it when people are in our house and they ask, "Do you have a rest room?"
I always want to say, "No, we just go in the back yard and dig a hole."

Two cannibals are eating lunch together.
One says, "I don't like my mother-in-law."
The other says, "Just eat the vegetables."

HOW I LEARNED TO MIND MY OWN BUSINESS:
Walking past the mental hospital, I hear a chorus of "13 … 13… 13 …" The fence is too high but I see a hole and put my eye to it. Someone pokes my eye with a stick and they all chant "14 … 14 … 14…"

Stephen Wright says when he dies, he's leaving his body to science-fiction.

YOU'RE TOO OLD TO TRICK OR TREAT WHEN...

You keep knocking on your own front door.

A candy bar dropped into your bag makes you lose your balance and fall over.

People say "Great mask," but you're not wearing a mask.

When the door opens, often you yell, "Trick or..." and then can't remember the rest.

You have to carefully choose a costume that doesn't dislodge your hairpiece.

You're the only Power Ranger in the neighborhood with a walker.

You have to go home often to pee.

A BEAUTIFUL POEM ABOUT GROWING OLDER

Crap...I forgot the words.

Wife: There's a problem with the car. It has water in the carburetor.
Husband: Water in the carburetor? That's ridiculous.
Wife: I tell you it's true.
Husband: You don't even know what a carburetor is. Where's the car?
Wife: In the swimming pool.

Doctor says to woman, "Madam, your husband needs a rest and some peace. So here are some sleeping pills."
Wife asks, "When should he take them?"
Doctor says, "They're for you!"

A new client had just come in to see a famous lawyer.
"How much do you charge?" asked the new client. "I charge $200 to answer three questions."
"Well, that's a bit steep, isn't it?"
"Yes, it is," said the lawyer. "And your third question?"

Getting old is when you see a really old penny and discover it was minted in your birth year.

When I was a kid, nap time was like a punishment. Now, as a grownup, it's a small vacation.

I think, therefore I'm single.

A man and his wife were in the process of getting a divorce in a local court in Greece; but the custody of the children proved an ongoing problem. The mother jumped to her feet and protested to the judge that since she had brought the children into this world, she should retain custody of them.

The judge then asked the man for his side. "Your Honor," he said, after some thought, "when I put a coin into a vending machine and a bottle of soda comes out, does the bottle belong to me or to the machine?" DON'T LAUGH ... HE WON!

I have finally discovered what's wrong with my brain. On the left side there is nothing right. On the right side there's nothing left.

When someone tells you to get a grip, apparently around their neck is not what they meant.

Last year, I joined a support group for procrastinators. We haven't met yet!

I remember the words to every song from the 70s but I forgot why the hell I came into this room.

Two older women:
"My memory is so bad."
"How bad is it?"
"How bad is what?"

Teach your daughters how to shoot.
Because a restraining order is just a piece of paper.

THE GEEZER TEST
How many of these do you remember?

- Cap guns
- Home milk deliveries in glass bottles
- TV test patterns early in the morning
- Stamp books and redemption centers
- Phone booths
- Aluminum ice-cube trays with pull handles
- Subway tokens

- Crazy Eddie's
- Earl Sheib's auto paint jobs
- Free road maps at service stations
- Seltzer bottles
- Doctors who made house calls
- Cigarette vending machines
- Flash cubes
- Johnny on the Pony; running bases; stoop ball; Lincoln Logs
- F. W. Woolworth Company
- Checker cabs

If you remember more than ten, you are officially a geezer

A virgin birth, I can believe...
But three wise men?

Love is a merry little elf who dances a jig, then turns on you with a machine gun.

My idea of housework is to sweep the room with a glance.

Marriage isn't a word. It's a sentence.

Marriage has no guarantees. If that's what you're looking for, go live with a car battery.

The best way to keep the kids at home is to make the home atmosphere pleasant—and let the air out of the tires.

Nothing needs changing more than your neighbor's habits.

I failed to make the chess team because of my height.

Two can live as cheaply as one can play golf.

First guy: My wife's an angel!
Second guy: You're lucky! Mine's still alive!

The big status symbol today is a smart phone clipped onto belt or purse. I can't afford one, so I'm wearing my garage door opener.

I spent a fortune on cologne and clothes before I realized that people just didn't like me.

What if we put pictures of missing husbands on beer cans? I bet we'd find a few.

When people see the cat's litter box, they always say, "Oh, you have a cat?"
Just once, I want to say, "No, it's for company. Hop right in!"

I have that dreaded furniture disease.
That's when your chest is falling into your drawers.

Birds of a feather flock together ... and then crap on your car.

The older you get, the tougher it is to lose.

Did you ever notice that the Roman numerals for 40 are XL?

I was thinking about how people seem to read the Bible a whole lot more as they get older. Then it dawned on me: they're cramming for their finals.

In the emergency application at the doctor's office, when they ask who should be contacted in case of emergency, I always write, "An ambulance!"

Take my advice; I don't use it anyway.

If you can smile when things go wrong, you have someone in mind to blame.

He who hesitates... is probably right.

The easiest way to find something that's lost in the house is to buy a replacement.

The most important purpose of a child's middle name is so he'll know when he's really in trouble.

A penny saved is a government oversight.

Eventually you reach the point when you stop lying about your age and start bragging about it.

Being young is nice but old is comfortable.

When you want to go back to your youth... think of algebra.

You know you are getting old when everything either dries up or leaks.

At my age, rolling out of bed in the morning is easy. Getting up off the floor is another story.

GOO.GLE.HEI.MER'S: When you think of something you want to look up, and forget what it when you get to the computer.

My sex life is like my Ferrari.
I don't have a Ferrari.

I'm old enough to make my own decisions... just not young enough to remember what I decided.

In a little while, I plan to tell my grandsons that I am older than the internet; that should blow their minds forever.

I figure I'm not really OLD... I've just been young for a long time.

I hate it when ugly people say, "I need my beauty sleep." I want to say to them, "Forget that. You need to hibernate."

A recent newspaper article reported that a woman has sued St. Luke's Hospital, saying that after her husband was treated there, he lost all interest in sex.
A hospital spokesman replied: "Mr. Smith was admitted into Ophthalmology. All we did was correct his eyesight."

Good health is the slowest way to die.

Two middle-aged Wisconsin men are out on a lake, fishing and drinking beer. Very quietly, one says, "I think I'm going to divorce my wife. She hasn't spoken to me in over two months."
His friend sips thoughtfully at his beer, then says, "Better think it over, buddy. Women like that are hard to find."

I changed my car horn to the sound of gunshots. People move out of the way much quicker now.

My husband and I divorced over religious differences. He thought he was God and I didn't.

At the bank, I told the teller, "I'd like to open a joint account."
"Fine," she said. "Who with?"
"Anyone with lots of money."

Seeing a spider isn't a problem. The problem begins when it disappears.

I don't like making plans for the day because then the word "premeditated" gets thrown around in the courtroom.

Employer to applicant: In this job, we need someone who is responsible.
Applicant: I'm the one you want, then. On my last job, every time anything went wrong they said I was responsible.

Doctor to patient: I have some bad news and some very bad news.
Patient to doctor: Well, give me the bad news first.
Doctor: The lab called with your test results. You have 24 hours to live.
Patient: 24 HOURS! That's terrible! What could be worse news than that!
Doctor: I've been trying to reach you since yesterday.

What do you call a lawyer gone bad?
A Senator.

It's easier to get older than wiser.

I heard a guy complaining about how expensive his wedding is. He is going to be real pissed when he finds out how much divorce is going to cost.

LIFE: Available for a limited time only. Limit one (1) per person. Subject to change without notice. Provided "as is" and without any warranties. Nontransferable and is the sole responsibility of the recipient. May incur damages arising from use or misuse. Additional parts sold separately. Your mileage may vary. Subject to all applicable fees and taxes. Terms and conditions apply.

MAN: In the moonlight, your teeth look just like pearls.
WOMAN: Who's Pearl, and what were you doing in the moonlight with her?

After a certain age, if you don't wake up aching somewhere... you may be dead.

I have the body of a god: Buddha.

A little old lady calls her neighbor on the phone. "Please come and help me with a jigsaw puzzle. I just can't figure out how to start it."
The neighbor comes over, looks at the box and the pieces spread out on the table and the old lady says, "According to the picture on the box... this is supposed to be a rooster."
Taking her hand, the neighbor says, "First, no matter what we do, we cannot assemble these pieces into the picture of a rooster. Second, let's relax and have a cup of tea and then... let's put all the cornflakes back in the box."

I really think that tossing and turning in bed at night should be considered exercise.

Since the weather's been so bad, I've put off spring cleaning until next year.

Next year, I'm going to move in with my kids, hog the computer, pay no bills, eat all the food, trash the house, and—when asked to clean up--I'll pitch a fit like that would kill me!

Of course I talk to myself.
Sometimes I need expert advice.

My brain is like the Bermuda Triangle.
Information goes in and is never seen again.

When I die, I want my last words to be: "I left a million dollars in cash under the ---"

Aging seems to be the only available way to live a longer life.

I have a hard time deciphering the fine line between hunger and boredom.

My people skills are just fine. It's my tolerance for idiots that needs work.

A man hasn't been feeling well, so he goes to his doctor for a complete checkup. Afterwards the doctor walks in with the results.

"I'm afraid I have some very bad news. You're dying and you don't have much time left."

"Oh, that's terrible!" cries the man. "Give it to me straight, Doc. How long have I got?"

"Ten," the doctor says sadly.

"Ten?" says the man. "Ten what? Months? Weeks? Days?"

"Nine..."

My girlfriend and I went to the local bar for some beers and the idiots there kept jeering and calling me "pedophile," just because I'm 50 and she's 21. It completely spoiled our tenth anniversary celebration.

The kids text me "plz" which is shorter than "please." I text back "no" which is shorter than "yes."

A minister parked his car in a no-parking space in New York City. He put a note under the windshield wiper that said: I have circled the block 10 times. If I don't park here, I'll miss my appointment with the Bishop. Forgive us our trespasses."
When he returned he found a parking ticket and this note: "I've circled this block for ten years. If I don't give you a ticket, I'll lose my job. Lead us not into temptation."

Lord, grant me the strength to accept the things I cannot change, the courage to change the things I can and the friends to post my bail when I finally snap.

I'm going to retire and live off my savings. Not sure what I'll do that second week.

Oops! Did I roll my eyes out loud?

The biggest lie I tell myself?
"I don't need to write that down. I'll remember it."

My wife and I were sitting at a table at her high school reunion and she kept staring at a drunken man swigging his drink as he sat alone at a nearby table.

I asked her, "Do you know him?"

"Yes," she sighed. "He's my old boyfriend...I understand he started drinking right after we split up many years ago, and I hear he hasn't been sober since."

"My God!" I said, "Who would think a person could go on celebrating that long"

I like long walks, especially when they are taken by people who annoy me.

I saw a woman wearing a sweat shirt with "Guess" on it. So I said "Implants?" Then she gave me a black eye.

Your kids are becoming you.
Now that I'm older I thought it was great that I seemed to have more patience.
Turns out I just don't give a shit.

THE IMPORTANCE OF WALKING

Walking can add minutes to your life. This enables you at 85 years old to spend an additional four months in a nursing home at $5,000 per month.

My grandfather started walking 5 miles a day when he was 60. Now, he's 95 and we have no idea where the hell he is.

You know you're a senior citizen when every time you leave your house, you have to go back because of something you forgot.

TODAY IS THE OLDEST YOU'VE EVER BEEN, YET THE YOUNGEST YOU'LL EVER BE.

Going out is good... Coming home is better!

YOU KNOW YOU'RE OLD WHEN...

You forget names, but it's OK because other people forgot they even knew you.

The things you used to care to do you no longer care to do, but you really do care that you don't care to do them anymore.

You sleep better in a lounge chair with the TV blaring than in a bed. It's called "pre-sleep".

You miss the days when everything worked with an "ON" and "OFF" switch.

You tend to use more 4 letter words... "What?" "When?" Where?"

What used to be freckles are now liver spots

You have 3 sizes of clothes in your closet...2 of which you will never wear.

My wife told me she was like a fine wine— getting better with age. So I locked her in the cellar.

Let me get this straight...women can have fake hair, nails, lashes, breasts, lips, and ass ...but want a real man?

Two men knocked on my front door today and asked if I would donate to the new local swimming pool. So I gave them a bottle of water.

Two elderly gentlemen were sitting on a bench when one says to the other,
"Joe, I'm 85 years old and I'm just full of aches and pains. I know you're about my age. How do you feel?
Joe says, "I feel just like a newborn baby."
"Really, like a newborn baby?"
"Yes, No hair, No teeth and I think I just wet my pants."

I put the "un" in predictable.

I was at the bank last week, when an old lady asked me to check her balance...So I pushed her over.

After an argument with my wife, I like to tighten the lids on all the jars. Just so I can say, "Oh? You need me now?"

A college student challenged a senior citizen, saying it was, "impossible for their generation to understand today's generation. It was a different world. Today we have TV, jet planes, space travel, computers..."
At a pause in the student's litany, the old guy said, "You're right. We didn't have those things, so we invented them. What are you doing for the next generation?"

This wise-guy looked at my beer belly last night and sarcastically said, "Is that Corona or Bud?"
I said, "There's a tap underneath, taste it and find out."

I was telling a woman in a bar about my ability to guess what day a woman was born by feeling her breasts.

"Really" she said, "Go on then...try."
After about 30 seconds of fondling, she began to lose patience and said, "Come on, What day was I born?'
I said, "Yesterday."

I was in a bar last night and saw a fat chick dancing on a table.
I said, "Nice legs."
The girl giggled and said with a smile, "Do you really think so?"
I said, "Definitely, most tables would have collapsed by now."

After 45 years of hard work, a man retired with $5,000,000.which he had gained through courage, diligence, shrewd investments, devotion to duty, And the death of an uncle who left him $4,999,999.

A senior citizen said to his eighty year old buddy, "I hear you're getting married?"
"Yep," said the friend.
"Do I know her?"

"Nope."

"This woman, is she good looking?'

"Not really."

Is she a good cook?"

"No, she can't cook too well."

Does she have a lot of money?"

"Nope, poor as a church mouse."

"Well then is she good in bed?"

"I don't know."

"Why in the world do you want to marry her then?"

"Because she can still drive."

I took my wife to a new restaurant. The waiter for some reason took my order first.

"I'll have the rump steak, rare please."

He said, "Aren't you worried about the mad cow?"

"Nah, she can order for herself.

I recently picked a new primary care doctor. After two visits and exhaustive lab tests, he said I was doing "Fairly well for my age."

(I just turned seventy-five).

A little concerned about that comment, I couldn't resist asking him, "Do you think I'll live to be 80?"

He asked, "Do you smoke weed, or drink beer, wine or hard liquor?"

"Oh no," I replied. "And I'm not doing drugs"

Then he asked, "Do you eat Porterhouse steaks and barbecued ribs?"

I said, "Sometimes...my former doctor said that all red meat is very unhealthy!"

"Do you spend a lot of time in the sun, for example playing golf, boating, sailing, hiking, or bicycling?"

"NO I don't," I said...

He looked at me and said, "Then why do you even care?"

Bob, a 70-year-old wealthy widower shows up at the Country Club with a breathtakingly beautiful and very sexy 25-year-old blonde who impresses every one with her youthful charm and sex appeal. She hangs over Bob's arm and listens intently to his every word.

His buddies at the Club are all aghast. They corner him and ask, "Bob how did you get this trophy girlfriend?"

Bob replies, "Girlfriend, she's my wife!"

They ask, "How did you persuade her to marry you?"

"I lied about my age," Bob says.

"Did you tell her you were only 50?"

Bob smiles and says, "No, I told her I was 90."

After she woke up, a woman told her husband, "I dreamed that you gave me a pearl necklace. What do you think it means?"

"You'll know tonight," he said. That evening, he gave her a package. Delighted, she opened it – to find a book entitled, "The Meaning of Dreams."

A group of Americans were travelling by tour bus through Switzerland. They stopped at a Cheese Farm and a young guide led them through the process of cheese making. She told them that goat's milk was used, and showed them a lovely hillside where many goats were grazing.

"These," she explained, "are the older goats put out to pasture when they no longer produce. What do you do in America with your old goats?"

A spry old gentleman answered, "They send us on bus tours."

Bob stood over his tee shot for what seemed like forever. He waggled, looked up, looked down, waggled again but didn't start his back swing.

Finally, his exasperated partner asked, "What the hell is taking so long?"

"My wife is up there watching me from the club house," said Bob. "I want to make a perfect shot."

Finally, his partner responded, "You'll never hit her from here."

I was raised as an only child, which really pissed off my sister.

QUESTIONS AND ANSWERS FROM THE AARP

Q. How can you improve the heart rate of a 65-year-old husband?
A. Tell him you're pregnant.

Q. What can a man do while his wife is going through menopause?
A. Keep busy. If you're handy, you can finish the basement. When you're done you'll have a place to live.

Q. Where can men over the age of 60 find younger women who are interested in them?
A. Try a bookstore under fiction.

Q. How can you avoid wrinkles?
A. Take off your glasses.

Q. Why should older people use valet parking?
A.Valets don't forget where they park your car.
Q. Is it common for 60–plus people to have problems with short term memory?
A. Memory isn't the problem, retrieving it is.

Q. As people age, do they sleep more soundly?
A.Yes, but usually in the afternoon.

Q.Where should Seniors look for their glasses?
A. On their foreheads.

Q. What is the most common remark made by seniors when they enter antique stores?
A. "I remember these."

A little old man shuffled slowly into an ice cream parlor and pulled himself slowly and painfully up onto a stool. After catching his breath, he ordered a banana split.
The waitress asked kindly, "Crushed nuts?"
"No," he replied. "Arthritis."

FUN (AND FUNNY) FACTS

When a man and woman marry, they become as one. Later on, they discover who won.

A picture is now worth only 210 words.

If you're going to teach your children the value of a dollar... do it quick!

The two most common elements in the known universe are hydrogen and stupidity.

Breathe in. Breathe out. Breathe in. Breathe out. Forget that and attaining Enlightenment will be the least of your problems.

Married men say they do the following twice as often as when they were single: change their underwear.

An egotist is someone who is more interested in himself than in me.

He who laughs, lasts.

A day without sunshine is like a day in Seattle.

I intend to live forever. So far, so good.

A gossip is someone with a great sense of rumor.

Middle age is when your burn the midnight oil at about 9:00 PM.

War doesn't determine who is right, only who is left.

Starfish don't have brains.

The strongest muscle in the human body is the tongue.

Butterflies taste with their feet.

Law of life: you can't fall off the floor.

Polar bears are left-handed.

At the time of the first space flights, NASA found that ballpoint pens wouldn't work under zero-gravity conditions. They spent six years and millions of dollars to design a pen that would work under virtually any condition.
The Russians used a pencil.

A glass that is holding 50% air and 50% water is, technically, completely full.

If there are no ups and downs in your life... it means you are dead.

In the 1600s, people used urine to tan animal skins.
Many families would all pee into the same pot and the pot was taken to the tannery once a day, where it was bought. If you had to do this in order to survive, you were "piss poor."
But worse than that was being in a family that couldn't afford an extra pot. Then, you "didn't have a pot to piss in" and were the poorest of the poor.

Bread was divided according to status. Workers got the burnt bottom, the family got the middle, and guests were given the top, or upper crust.

The floor in most homes was dirt, hence the saying, "dirt poor." The well-to-do had slate floor that would get slippery in the wet weather. So they spread thresh (straw) on the floor to soak up the water. As the winter wore on, more thresh was added and when you opened the door, it would all come sliding out. A piece of wood was placed at the entry, and was called a threshold.

There was a time when people noticed scratch marks on the insides of coffins. People had been buried alive! People then tied a string around the corpse's wrist, led it through the coffin lid, and tied it to a bell. Someone would sit in the graveyard all night (graveyard shift) and listen for the bell of a "dead ringer."

"Dammit, I'm mad" is "Dammit, I'm mad" spelled backwards.

The Middle Ages had many pitfalls. Lead cups were used for ale or whisky. The combination would sometimes knock the imbibers out for a couple of days. Someone walking along the road might take an unconscious man for dead and the man's family would prepare him for burial. The body was laid out on the kitchen table for several days and the family would gather around, eating and drinking, waiting to see if he would wake up. From this we get the custom of holding a wake.

The sentence "the quick brown fox jumps over the lazy dog" uses every letter of the alphabet.

The words "racecar," "kayak," and "level" are palindromes: words that read the same whether read backwards or forwards.

The longest word that can be typed using only one row of keys is "typewriter."

A cat has 32 muscles in each ear.

Goldfish have a memory span of three seconds.

A "jiffy" is an actual unit of time: 1/100 of a second.

Sharks are the only fish that can blink with both eyes.

A snail can sleep for three years.

Almonds are part of the peach family.

An ostrich's eye is bigger than its brain.

February 1865 is the only month in recorded history not to have a full moon.

Babies are born without kneecaps. They don't appear until the child is 2-6 years old.

In the last 4,000 years, no new animals have been domesticated.

Rubber bands last longer if refrigerated.

The microwave was invented after a researcher walked by a radar tube and a chocolate bar melted in his pocket.

The winter of 1932 was so frigid that Niagara Falls froze completely solid.

Married life is very frustrating. In the first year of marriage, the man speaks and the woman listens. In the second year of marriage, the woman speaks and the man listens. In the third year of marriage, they both speak and the neighbors listen.

SCIENTIFIC CONVERSIONS WITH A DIFFERENCE

The ratio of an igloo's circumference to its diameter:
Eskimo pi.

2,000 lbs of Chinese soup: won ton.

One millionth of a mouthful of mouthwash: One microscope.

Time between slipping on a peel and smacking the pavement: one bananosecond.

16.5 feet in the Twilight Zone: one rod serling.

Half of a large intestine: one semicolon.

One million aches: one megahertz.

Basic unit of laryngitis: one hoarse-power.

Four nickels: 2 paradigms.

453.6 graham crackers: one pound cake

One million microphones: one megaphone.

365.25 days on wheels: one unicycle.

2,000 mockingbirds: 2 kilomockingbirds.

52 cards: one decacards.

One kilo of falling figs: one FigNewton.

1,000 milliliters of wet socks: one literhosen.

1/1,000,000 of a fish: one microfiche.

One trillion pins: one terrapin.

10 rations: one decoration.

100 rations: one C-ration.

Weight an evangelist carries with God: one billi-gram.

2.4 statute miles of intravenous surgical tubing at Yale University Hospital: one I V League.

Two monograms: one diagram.

Time it takes to sail 220 yards at one nautical mile per hour: knotfurlong.

HOW GOVERNMENT BUREAUCRATS KEEP THEIR JOBS:

Pythagorean theorem..........................24 words

Lord's prayer..66 words

Archimedes' Principle............................67 words

Ten Commandments..........................179 words

Gettysburg Address..........................286 words

Declaration of Independence......1,300 words

U.S. Constitution..........................7,818 words

U.S. Government regulations on sale of cabbage:……………………………..26,911 words

This puts things in perspective, doesn't it?

The ocean liner QE2 moves only six inches for each gallon of diesel fuel that it burns.

Our eyes are always the same size from birth; but our ears and nose never stop growing.

The average person's left hand does 56% of the work when typing.

There are more chickens than people on planet Earth.

Winston Churchill was born in a ladies' room during a dance.

Only four words in English end in "dous:" tremendous, horrendous, stupendous and hazardous.

Women blink nearly twice as much as men.

Two words in English have all five vowels in order: abstemious and facetious.

Leonardo Da Vinci invented the scissors.

Peanuts are one of the ingredients in dynamite.

After marriage, husband and wife become like two sides of a coin: they just can't face each other, but they still are stuck together.

No matter how much you may care, some people are just losers.

All the ants in Africa weigh more than all the elephants in Africa.

I started out with nothing—and I still have most of it.

My wild oats are mostly enjoyed with prunes and all-bran, these days.

I finally got my head together and now my body is falling apart.

TOP THINGS ONLY WOMEN UNDERSTAND

The difference between beige, ecru, cream, off-white, linen white, and eggshell.

Eyelash curlers.

The inaccuracy of every bathroom scale.

Cat's facial expression.

The need for the same style of shoes in different colors.

Taking a car trip without trying to beat your best time.

Why bean sprouts are not just weeds.

And the number one fact only women get:
OTHER WOMEN.

Funny, I don't remember being absent-
minded.

If all is not lost, then where the heck is it?

I wish the buck really did stop here. I could
use a few of them.

It was a whole lot easier to get older than to
get wiser.

It's hard to make a comeback when you
haven't been anywhere.

The world only beats a path to your door
when you're in the bathroom.

It's not hard meeting expenses; they're
everywhere.

It takes years to build up trust, and it only takes suspicion, not proof, to destroy it.

It takes glass one million years to decompose, which means it never wears out.

We are responsible for what we do—unless we are celebrities.

FUN FACTS FOR EACH STATE OF THE UNION

ALABAMA: In l968, the first place to have 9-1-1 phone service.

ALASKA: One out of 64 people has a pilot's license.

ARIZONA: the only state in the lower 48 that does not follow Daylight Savings Time.

ARKANSAS: has the only active diamond mine in the U.S.

CALIFORNIA: An economy so large that if it were a country, it would rank seventh in the world.

COLORADO: In 1976, it became the only state to turn down the Olympics.

CONNECTICUT: The Frisbee was invented here at Yale University.

DELAWARE: has more scientists and engineers than any other state.

FLORIDA: Jacksonville is the largest city in the U.S.

GEORGIA: It was here, in 1886, that pharmacist John Pemberton made the first vat of Coca Cola.

HAWAII: where people live, on average, five years longer than residents in any other state.

IDAHO: Television was invented in Rigby in 1922.

ILLINOIS: The most corrupt state in the union, with one governor in jail and one pending jail.

INDIANA: Home to Santa Claus, which gets half a million letters to Old Nick every year.

IOWA: the only state that begins with two vowels.

KANSAS: has an exact replica of the house in the Wizard of Oz.

KENTUCKY: has more than $6 billion in gold underneath Fort Knox.

LOUISIANA: has parishes instead of counties because they were originally Spanish church units.

MAINE: So big, it covers as many square miles as the other five New England states combined.

MARYLAND: The Ouija board was created in Baltimore in 1892

MASSACHUSETTS: the fig newton is named after Newton, MA.

MICHIGAN: Fremont, home to Gerber, is the baby food capital of the world.

MINNESOTA: Bloomington's Mall of America is so big, if you spend ten minutes in each store, you'd be there for nearly four days.

MISSISSIPPI: Because President Teddy Roosevelt refused to shoot a bear here, toy bears were ever after called teddy bears.

MISSOURI: birthplace of the ice cream cone.

MONTANA: a sapphire from Montana is in the Crown Jewels of England.

NEBRASKA: More triplets are born here.

NEW HAMPSHIRE: birthplace of Tupperware, invented by Earl Tupper in 1938.

NEW JERSEY: has the most shopping malls.

NEW MEXICO: Smokey the Bear was rescued from a 1950 forest fire.

NEW YORK: home to the nation's oldest cattle ranch, started in 1747 in Montauk.

NORTH CAROLINA: Home of Krispy Kreme donuts.

NORTH DAKOTA: Rigby, N.D. is the exact geographical center of North America.

OHIO: The hot dog was invented here.

OKLAHOMA: The grounds of the state capitol are covered by operational oil wells.

OREGON: Has the most ghost towns in the country.

PENNSYLVANIA: The smiley ☺ was first used by computer scientists at Carnegie Mellon University.

RHODE ISLAND: The nation's oldest bar, The White Horse Tavern, opened here in 1673.

SOUTH CAROLINA: Sumpter Country is home to the world's largest gingko farm.

SOUTH DAKOTA: is the only state that's never had an earthquake.

TENNESSEE: Nashville's Grand Ole Opry is the longest-running live radio show in the world.

TEXAS: Dr. Pepper was invented in Waco in 1885.

UTAH: The first Kentucky Fried Chicken opened here in 1952.

VERMONT: Montpelier is the only state capitol without a McDonald's.

VIRGINIA: Home of the world's largest office building, the Pentagon.

WASHINGTON: Seattle has twice as many college grads as any other state.

WASHINGTON, D.C.: first planned capitol anywhere.

WEST VIRGINIA: world's first brick-paved street.

WISCONSIN: Home to the inventor of the ice-cream sundae.

WYOMING: The first state to allow women to vote.

ONE STATE IS MISSING FROM THE LIST! Do you know which one? (Answer on page 331)

Your tongue is the only muscle in your body that is attached at only one end.

Each year, two million smokers either quit smoking or die of tobacco-related diseases.

Gold is the only metal that doesn't rust, even if it's buried in the ground for thousands of years.

Zero is the only number that cannot be represented by Roman numerals.

During the American Civil War, kites were used to deliver letters and newspapers.

Drinking water after eating reduces the acid in your mouth by 61%.

The song Auld Lang Syne is sung at the stroke of midnight in almost every English-speaking country in the world to bring in the new year. Auld Lang Syne means Old Times Past.

Nine out of every ten living things live in the ocean.

The tooth is the only part of the human body that cannot heal itself.

The University of Alaska system spans four time zones.

Warner Communications paid $28 million for the copyright to the Happy Birthday song.

The banana cannot reproduce itself. It can be propagated only by the hand of man.

Intelligent people have more zinc and copper in their hair.

If you can get into the bottom of a well or a tall chimney and look up, you will see stars, even in the middle of a bright day.

Caffeine increases the power of aspirin and other painkillers.

A comet's tail always points away from the sun.

The military salute evolved from medieval times, when knights in armor raised their visors to reveal their identity.

Avocados have the highest calories of any fruit.

Each year, the moon moves 2 inches away from the Earth.

Due to earth's gravity, it is impossible for mountains to be higher than 15,000 meters.

Strawberries are the only fruit that grow with their seeds on the outside.

It is said that line dancing was started by women waiting to use the bathroom.

The letter "J" does not appear anywhere on the periodic table of the elements.

I think I'm living in a haunted house. Every time I look in the mirror, this old lady comes and stands in front of me and blocks out my reflection.

The most memorable people in your life will be the friends who loved you even when you weren't very lovable.

I've decided that dryer lint is the cremated remains of all of my missing socks.

Once you lick the frosting off a cupcake, it becomes a muffin and we all know that muffins are healthy.

When we die, hearing is the last sense to go.

The earth gets 100 tons heavier every day due to falling space dust.

Soldiers do not march in step when going across a bridge. They could set up a vibration which could be strong enough to make the bridge collapse.

For every extra kilo carried on a space flight, 530 kilograms more fuel are required.

Dolphins are so intelligent that within a few weeks of captivity, they can train a man to stand on the edge of their pool and throw them fish three times a day.

Everything weighs one percent less at the equator.

If you help someone when they're in trouble, they will remember you when they're in trouble again.

SIMPLE TRUTH #1
Lovers help each other undress before sex. However, after sex, they always dress on their own. In this life, nobody helps you once you're screwed.

SIMPLE TRUTH #2
When a woman is pregnant, her friends touch her belly and say "Congratulations." But none of them touch the father's penis and say, "Good job."
Hard work is never appreciated.

In ancient times, strangers shook hands to show they were unarmed.

314 backwards spells PIE
Forgive your enemy but remember the bastard's name.

If you lift a kangaroo's tail off the ground, it cannot hop.

You can't snore and dream simultaneously.

A HISTORY OF SAYINGS WE OFTEN USE

BUYING THE FARM: this is synonymous with dying. During WWI, soldiers were given life insurance policies worth $5,000. This was about the price of an average farm, so if you died, you "bought the farm" for your surviving family.

PASSING THE BUCK/THE BUCK STOPS HERE: In the early West, most men carried a jackknife made by the Buck company. When playing poker, it was common to place one if front of the dealer. When there was a new dealer, he was given the deck of cards and a knife. If he didn't want to deal, he would "pass the Buck" to the next player and if that player accepted, "the Buck stopped there."

SHIP STATEROOMS: Passenger cabins on steamboats were not numbered, but named after states, and to this day are called "staterooms."

COBWEBS: Simple. The Old English word for sider was "cob."

HOT OFF THE PRESS: As paper goes through a rotary printing press, the paper gets hot. If you grab the paper right off the press, it is both hot and contains the most immediate information.

A SHOT OF WHISKY: In the Old West, a .45 cartridge for a six-shooter cost 12 cents, as did a small glass of whisky. If a cowhand was low on cash, he would trade a small cartridge for a "shot" and the small glass became known as a shot glass, as it still is.

BARGE IN: Heavy freight was moved along the Mississippi in large clumsy barges pushed by steamboats. They were almost impossible to control and would often swing into piers or other boats without warning, much like an unwelcome visitor who "barges in."

HOGWASH (meaning useless or worthless): When steamboats would carry people and animals, pigs were washed before being put on board. The mud and filth washed off became totally useless water, or "hogwash."

SHOWBOAT: These were floating theaters built on a barge pushed along a river by a steamboat. They were decorated in especially gaudy manner to get attention, which we today call "showboating."

Answer to missing state is NEVADA

HILARIOUS ONE LINERS

SLIGHTLY LONGER JOKES

Says one husband to the other: "My wife's female intuition is so finely tuned; she often knows I'm wrong before I've even opened my mouth."

My wife was standing in front of the bedroom mirror, in the nude. She was obviously not happy with what she saw and she said to me, "I feel horrible. I look old, fat, and ugly. I really need you to pay me a compliment." So I said, "Your eyesight's pretty damn near perfect."

We should limit all politicians to two terms: one in office and one in prison. It works. Detroit and Chicago already do this.

A man returns from a morning of fishing and decides to take a nap. He looks so relaxed that his wife decides she'll take the boat out. She goes a short distance, then anchors and takes out a book.
Along comes a Game Warden in his boat. "Morning ma'am," he says, pulling alongside. "What are you doing?"
"Reading a book," she says.
"You're in a restricted fishing area."

"I'm sorry, but I'm not fishing, I'm reading."
"Yes, but I see you have all the equipment.
For all I know you could start up at any
moment. I'll have to take you in and write
you up."
"But I'm just reading," she says and the
entire conversation is repeated.
"If you take me in and write me up, Officer,
I'll have to charge you with sexual assault."
"But I haven't even touched you!"
"True. But you have all the equipment and
for all I know you could start at any
moment."
"Have a nice day, ma'am," he said as he
left.

Driving past Home Depot, our 2-year-old
screams, "Look, Mommy! Hos!"
Startled, I checked and sure enough there
were two very trashy looking women
walking out of the store.
I had about two minutes of a panic attack
before I realized the store was having a
massive sale on hoses a few feet from the
girls. There were about 200 blue hoses
lined up in front of the store.

Last night, my best friend and I were chatting in my living room and I said to her, "I know I can trust you. So I'm asking you: if I am ever in a vegetative state, dependent on some machine and fluids from a bottle, please, just pull the plug." So she got up, disconnected my computer and threw out the rest of my bottle of wine!

The entrance exam for medical school asked the following question:
"Rearrange the letters P S E N I to spell out the part of the human body most useful when erect." Those who spelled SPINE became doctors. The rest are in Congress.

A man received this text from his neighbor: "I'm sorry, Bob. I've been riddled with guilt. I've been tapping your wife every day, night and day. I can't get any in our house but that's no excuse. I am sorry." Bob, betrayed and anguished, didn't stop to think, grabbed his hunting rifle and without a word, went into the bedroom and headed over to shoot his neighbor dead. A moment later, a second text came in: "Damn that autocorrect! I meant 'wifi' not wife!"

At a crowded bus stop in a Texas city, a woman waiting for the bus was wearing a tight leather skirt. When a bus stopped and it was her turn to get on, she realized that her skirt was too tight to allow her leg to come up to the first step. Slightly embarrassed and with a quick smile to the driver, she reached behind to unzip her skirt. It didn't work so she unzipped a little more. Once again, she was foiled and she unzipped yet again. A tall cowboy standing behind her picked her up easily by the waist and placed her gently on the top step. Embarrassed, she turned to the Good Samaritan and said, "How dare you touch me? I don't even know you!"
The cowboy smiled and drawled, "Well, normally I would agree with you. But after you unzipped my fly three times, I kinda figured we was friends."

Saturday morning, I got up early, dressed quietly, slipped downstairs, made my lunch and hooked the boat up to the van. Ah, a day of fishing! But when I backed the van out of the garage I saw that it was teeming

rain, and the radio said we could expect more of the same until tomorrow afternoon. So I went back into the house, put the lunch into the fridge, tiptoed upstairs, undressed quietly, and slid back into bed.
I cuddled up to my wife's back, now with a different anticipation. "The weather out there is terrible," I whispered in her ear.
My loving wife replied, "And can you believe my stupid husband is out fishing in that!"

The minister had a lot on his mind, and was annoyed to find that his organist was sick and a substitute had been brought in. The substitute asked what he should play. "Here's a copy of the service," said the minister. "But you'll have to think of something after I make an announcement about our need for money." At a pause in the service, the minister told the congregation, "Brothers and sisters, we are in great need. The roof repairs will cost $4,000. Any of you who can pledge $100 or more, please stand up."
At that moment, the organ struck up the national anthem. And that is how the substitute became the regular organist.

Stan was greeted after work by his wife, who was wearing a sexy little dress. "Have you ever seen a twenty dollar bill all crumpled up?" she asked. He said no, he hadn't.

She gave him a little smile, reached into her cleavage and pulled out a crumpled twenty. "Now," said she, "have you ever seen a fifty dollar bill all crumpled up?"

"No, I don't think so." He was intrigued.

She hiked up her skirt and pulled from the top of her pantyhose a crumpled fifty. "Now then, have you ever seen $50,000 dollars all crumpled up?"

He grinned. What in the world—?

"No, I don't believe I have," he played along.

The wife replied, "Go look in the garage..."

A guy came racing into a crowded bar, with a gun in his hand which he kept pointing this way and that. "I want to know," he bellowed, "who the hell has been sleeping with my wife?"

A voice from the back shouted: "I don't think you brought enough ammo!"

Rush hour. A traffic light turned yellow and a driver did the right thing, stopping at the crosswalk. A tailgating woman was furious. She honked her horn over and over, screaming in frustration, and wished him ill in several different ways. While she was still mid-rant, she heard a tap on her window and looked to see a police officer. He ordered her to exit her car with her hands up, and in spite of her protestations, took her to the precinct station. There, she was fingerprinted and her photo taken. She was then put in a holding cell. After a couple of hours, the cell door was unlocked and she was escorted back to the booking desk where the arresting officer was waiting with her personal effects. "I'm very sorry for the mistake," he said. "I pulled up behind you while you were blowing your horn, flipping off the guy in front of you and cursing a blue streak. I noticed the 'What Would Jesus Do' bumper sticker, the 'Choose Life' license plate, the 'Follow Me to Sunday School' bumper sticker and the chrome-plated Christian fish emblem on the trunk, so naturally... I assumed you had stolen the car."

Marie had been married over 60 years to a grouchy guy named Edwin. Nobody understood why she stayed with him. He complained about everything and if you talked back, he would say, "Never you mind. I'll be coming back to see you after I'm dead!" Everyone was scared of him.
Well, Edwin died and the neighbors all asked Marie, "Aren't you afraid he'll really come back to bother all of us after he's buried?" "Let him try!" said Marie. "I'm having him buried upside down and you know he'll never ever ask for directions!"

Sam Anderson was on his death bed with all his family gathered around him: his wife, Sylvia; his two sons, Bernie and Jake; and his daughter, Sybil. As he lay dying he said: "Bernie, you get all of the lower East Side. Jake, you'll take the West Village and you, Sybil, the East Village. Sylvia, you can have the entire downtown." Sam's nurse was impressed. She said to Sylvia, "Mr. Anderson must have been a very good businessman to own all those properties." "Properties, shmoperties," snapped Sylvia. "The shmuck has a seltzer route!"

341

They say that during sex, you burn off as many calories as running eight miles.
Who the hell runs eight miles in 15 seconds?

My spam folder is full of emails offering cheap Viagra. They must think I'm a soft target.

A psychiatrist was conducting a group therapy session with four young mothers and their small children.
"You all have obsessions," he observed.
"You, Marie, you're obsessed with eating. You've even named your daughter Candy."
He turned to the second mother. "Ann, your obsession is with money. Again, it manifests itself in your child's name, Penny."
He turned to the third mother. "Joyce your obsession is with alcohol. Your daughter's name is Brandy and your son's name is Chivas."
At this point, the fourth mother in the group quietly got up, took her little boy by the hand and whispered, "Come on, Dick. This guy has no idea what he's talking about. Let's pick up Peter and Willy from school and go get some dinner."

A motorist driving by a Texas ranch accidentally hit and killed a calf that was crossing the road.
The driver found the rancher and explained what had happened.
 "And I'm willing to pay fair compensation," he said.
"Well, that calf's worth about $200 today," said the rancher, "but in six years it would have been worth $900 and I believe that $900 would be fair compensation."
The motorist sat down and wrote a check for $900.
"Here," he said. "A check for $900. I've postdated it six years from now."

Yesterday, Bart had an appointment with the urologist for a prostate exam. He was understandably a bit nervous, and became even more so when he approached the receptionist's desk and found himself looking into a very angry face. He gave the receptionist his name. In an unnecessarily loud voice, the receptionist announced:
"YES, I HAVE YOUR NAME HERE. YOU WANT TO SEE THE DOCTOR ABOUT IMPOTENCE,

RIGHT?" All heads in the room snapped around to stare at a very embarrassed man. But Bart was no wuss and in an equally loud voice, he said, "NO, I'VE COME TO INQUIRE ABOUT A SEX-CHANGE OPEERATION, BUT I DON'T WANT THE SAME DOCTOR THAT DID YOURS."

After 30 years of marriage, a woman asked her husband to describe her. He gazed at her, then said, "You're A,B,C,D,E,F,G,H,I,J,K..."
"And that means?"
"Adorable. Beautiful. Cute. Delightful. Elegant. Fancy. Gorgeous. Honey."
Tears forming, she smiled, swallowed and said, "Oh, that's so lovely. But what about I, J and K?"
"I'm just kidding."

Sitting in a bar having drinks with an old friend, I casually pointed to two old guys sitting across the bar from us and said, "That's us in ten years, Joe."
He said, "That's a mirror, idiot!"

A visitor from the Netherlands was chatting with his American friend, jokingly explaining what the red, white and blue in his country's flag stood for. "Our flag symbolizes our taxes," said the man from the Netherlands. "We get red when we talk about them, white when we get our bill, and blue after we pay them." "That's the same with us," said the American. "Only we see stars, too."

A motorist, after getting stuck on a muddy road, paid a passing farmer five dollars to pull him out with his tractor.
After he was back on dry ground, he said to the farmer, "At those prices, I think you would be pulling people out of the mud day and night."
"Can't," replied the farmer. "At night I haul water for the hole."

My boss (who was out) called the office to ask if all was well. "All under control, although very busy," I said.
"Can you do me a favor?" my boss asked.
"Of course. What is it?" I said.
My boss replied: "Pick up the pace a little. I'm in the foursome behind you."

A man charged into the jewelry shop and removed a wristwatch from his pocket. "You said this watch would last a lifetime!" he shouted, "and it's already broken."
"Yes," said the jeweler. "But you looked pretty sick the day you bought it."

THE PROPER WAY TO CALL SOMEONE A BASTARD

A guy was getting ready to tee off on the first hole when a second golfer approached him and asked if they could play together. Although he preferred to play alone, he agreed.
They were even after the first few holes. Said the newcomer, "We seem evenly matched. How about playing for, say, five bucks a hole."
The first guy said he wasn't much for betting, but okay, why not.
The second player won the remaining sixteen holes with ease. As he was counting out his winnings, he confessed that he was the pro at a neighboring golf course and got his kicks from fooling other players.

The first fellow revealed that he was the parish priest.
The pro was flustered and apologetic.
He offered to return the money.
"You won fair and square," said the priest, "and I was foolish to bet with you. You keep your winnings."
The pro said, "Is there anything I can do to make it up to you?"
Said the priest,
"Well, you could come to Mass on Sunday and make a donation... And, if you bring your mother and father along... I'll marry them."

WOULD YOU MARRY AGAIN?

Husband and wife in bed, quietly reading.
Wife puts down her book.

WIFE: What would you do if I died? Would you get married again?

HUSBAND: Definitely not!

WIFE: Why not? Don't you like being married?

HUSBAND: In fact, I do like being married.

WIFE: Then why wouldn't you remarry?

HUSBAND: Okay, okay, I'd get married again.

WIFE: Would you live here in our house?

HUSBAND: I imagine so. Where else should we live?

WIFE: Would you sleep with her in our bed?

HUSBAND: Where else should we sleep?

WIFE: Would you give her my car to drive?

HUSBAND: Probably. It's almost new and it's a great car.

WIFE: Would you replace my pictures with hers?

HUSBAND: That would be the proper thing to do.

WIFE: Would you give her my jewelry?

HUSBAND: No, surely she'd prefer her own.

WIFE: Would you take her golfing with you?

HUSBAND: Yes, that's always a good time.

WIFE: Would she use my clubs?

HUSBAND: No, she's left-handed.

-silence-

HUSBAND: Crap...

The lawyer says, "I have good news and bad news." The CEO says, "I've had an awful day. Let's hear the good news first." Says the lawyer: "Your wife invested $20,000 in five pictures that are worth a minimum of two million." The CEO says enthusiastically, "Well done, that is very good news indeed! You've made my day! Now, what's the bad news?" "They are pictures of you in bed with your secretary."

I pulled into the crowded parking lot of our local shopping center one morning and rolled the windows halfway down to make sure there was enough air circulation for my new puppy. She was stretched out full length across the back seat and I wanted to impress upon her that she had to stay there. I walked backward to the curb, pointing my finger at the car and saying emphatically, "Now you stay! Do you hear me? Stay! Stay!"
The driver of a nearby car, a lovely young girl, gave me a strange look and said, "Why don't you just put it in PARK?"

I've finally learned that you cannot make someone love you.
All you can do is stalk them and hope they panic and give in.

Taking his seat in his chambers, the judge faced the opposing lawyers.
"So," he said, "I have been presented by both of you with a bribe."
Both lawyers squirmed uncomfortably.
"You, attorney Leon, gave me $15,000. And you, attorney Compos, gave me $10,000."

The judge reached into his pocket and pulled out a check, handing it to Leon.
"Now, then, I'm returning $5,000 and we're going to decide this case solely on the merits."

The boss and two managers, junior and senior, are on their way to a meeting when they all spot a magic lamp. They rub the lamp and a genie appears.
"Normally," says the genie, "each rub allows for three wishes but there are three of you, so... one each."
Senior manager says, "Me first! I want to be on a boat in the Bahamas with plenty of crew, food, and drink." Pffftt! And he was gone.
Junior manager says, "Send me to Florida to a beautiful condo with all the fixin's!" Pffftt! He's gone, too.
Calmly, the boss says, "I want those two idiots back in the office by 1:30 P.M."

I got caught taking a pee in the local swimming pool today.
The lifeguard shouted so loud, I nearly fell in.

A 20-something year-old girl finally decided to introduce her boyfriend to her parents. She hid him from them because she was afraid of how they'd react because he was very religious, but since they were engaged she couldn't hide it anymore. The boy shook the father's hand firmly and sat down for a talk.

"So I understand that you want to marry my daughter. Do you have a job to support her?"

"With God's help, sir, someday, yes."

"Are you planning on having kids?"

"With God's help, sir, someday, yes."

"I understand that you're a student. How are you going to pay your tuition and afford a baby?"

"With God's help, sir, I'm very certain both of these are possible goals."

The conversation went pleasantly and politely. After the boy left, the mother asked the father:

"Well, what do you think of the lad?"

To which the father replied:

"He seems pretty nice... the only problem is that he seems to believe that I'm God."

A factory foreman inspected a shipment of crystal vases leaving a plant, and approached his new packer. He put his arm around the man's shoulder.
"Well Sam, I see you did what I asked. Stamped the top of each box, 'This Side up, Handle with Care.'"
"Yes sir," the worker said. "And just to make sure, I stamped it on the bottom too."

While stitching a cut on the hand of a 75-year-old farmer, the doctor struck up a conversation with the old man. Eventually the topic got around to politicians and their role as our leaders.
The old farmer said: "Well, as I see it, most politicians are 'Post Tortoises.'"
Unfamiliar with the term, the doctor asked him what a 'Post Tortoise' was.
The old farmer explained, saying: "When you're driving down a country road and you come across a fencepost with a tortoise balanced on top, that's a Post Tortoise."
The old farmer saw the puzzled look on the doctor's face, so he continued to explain.
"You know he didn't get up there by himself. He doesn't belong up there. He's elevated

beyond his ability to function, and you just wonder what kind of idiot put him there to begin with."

Father O'Malley answers his phone.
"Hello, is this Father O'Malley?" someone asks.
"It is!"
"This is the IRS. Can you help us?"
"I can, yes."
"Do you know Ted Houlihan?"
"I do!"
"Is he a member of your congregation?"
"He is."
"Did he donate $10,000 to the church?"
"He will!"

A man wrote a letter to the IRS, saying, "I have been unable to sleep knowing that I have cheated on my income tax. I understated my taxable income and have enclosed a check for $200.00. If I still can't sleep, I will send the rest."

A woman was arrested for shoplifting. When she went before the judge, he asked her: "What did you steal?" She replied, "A can of

peaches." The judge asked her why she had stolen them and she replied that she was hungry. The judge then asked her how many peaches were in the can. She replied that there were 5. The judge then said, "I will give you 5 days in jail."
Before the judge could actually pronounce the punishment, the woman's husband spoke up and asked the judge if he could say something. The judge asked, "What is it?" The husband said, "She also stole a can of peas."

Two good ol' boys in an Alabama trailer park were sitting around talking one afternoon over a cold beer after getting off work from the local Auto plant. After a while, the first guy says to the second, "If'n I was to sneak over to your trailer Saturday and make love to your wife while you was off huntin' and she got pregnant and had a baby, would that make us kin?" The second guy scratched his head for a minute and squinted his eyes thinking very hard about the question. Finally, he says, "Well, I don't know about kin, but that would make us even!"

A very successful businessman had a meeting with his new son-in-law. "I welcome you into the family," said the man. "To show you how much we care for you, I am making you a 50-50 partner in my business. All you have to do is go to the factory every day and learn the operation."

The son-in-law interrupted. "I hate factories. I can't stand the noise!"

"I see," replied the father-in-law. "Well, then you'll work in the office and take charge of some of the operations."

"I hate office work," said the son-in-law. "I can't stand being stuck behind a desk!"

"Wait a minute," said the father-in-law. "I just made you half owner of a money-making industry, but you don't like factories and you won't work in an office. What am I going to do with you?"

"Easy," said the son-in-law. "Buy me out!"

A helicopter carrying passengers suddenly loses engine power and the aircraft begins to descend. The pilot safely performs an emergency landing in water, and tells the passengers to remain seated and to keep the doors closed, stating in emergency situations, the aircraft is designed to stay afloat for 30 minutes, giving rescuers time to arrive. Just then, a man gets out of his seat and runs over to open the door. The pilot screams at him, saying "Didn't you hear what I said? The aircraft is designed to stay afloat as long as the doors remain closed!" The passenger screams back, "Of course I heard you! But it's also designed to fly, and look how well that one worked out!"

During my prostate exam, I asked my doctor where I should put my pants. "Over there by mine" was NOT the answer I expected.

And old Italian man in Brooklyn is dying. He calls his grandson to his bedside and says to the boy, "Anthony, I wan' you to lissina me. I wan' you to take my chrome plated .38 revolver so you will always remember me."
"But Grandpa, I really don't like guns," says the boy. "How about you leave me your Rolex instead?"
"You lissina me, boy!" says the man. "Somma day you gonna be runna da business, you gonna have a beautiful wife,

lotsa money, a big-a home and maybe a couple of bambinos. Somma day you gonna come-a home and maybe finda your wife inna bed with another man. Whatta you gonna do then? Pointa to you watch and say, 'Times up!'"?

A visitor to Israel attended a recital and concert at the Moscovitz Auditorium. He was extremely impressed with the architecture and the acoustics. He inquired of the tour guide:
"Is this magnificent auditorium named after Chaim Moscovitz, the famed writer?"
"No," replied the tour guide. "It is named after Sam Moscovitz, the writer."
"Never heard of him," said the visitor. "What did he write?"
"A check," replied the guide.

6 DEADLY TERMS USED BY A WOMAN

1) FINE: This is the word women use to end an argument when she knows she is right and that you need to shut up.
2) NOTHING: This term means something, and you need to be worried.

3) GO AHEAD: This is a dare, not permission. Do not do it.
4) WHATEVER: A woman's way of saying "screw you."
5) THAT'S OKAY: She is thinking long and hard about how and when you will pay for your mistake.
6) WOW: This is not a compliment. She is amazed that one person could be so stupid.

LAWYER: Doctor, before you performed the autopsy, did you check for a pulse?

DOCTOR: No.

LAWYER: Did you check for blood pressure?

DOCTOR: No.

LAWYER: Did you check for breathing?

DOCTOR: No.

LAWYER: So, is it possible that the patient was still alive when you began the autopsy?

DOCTOR: No.

LAWYER: How can you be so sure, Doctor?

DOCTOR: His brain was in a jar on my desk.

LAWYER: But could the patient have still been alive, nonetheless?

DOCTOR: Yes, it is possible that he could have been alive and practicing law.

A man wants to become a magician so he goes out and buys a magic book. Later he gathers his family around the living room for his first trick. Reading his new book he reaches into a bag and pulls out a hammer. To the amazement of his family, the man hits himself on the head with it. He is unconscious and spends a month in the hospital. One day, a nurse notices the man's eyelids flutter. She calls the family in and they gather around his bed. Just then the man sits upright in bed, awake as can be and says... "TA-DAA!"

The mother of a 17-year-old girl was concerned that her daughter was having sex. Worried that she might become pregnant and adversely impact the family's reputation, she consulted with the family doctor. The doctor told her that teenagers are very willful and often rebel against their parents. He then told her to arrange for her daughter to be put on birth control and until then, to give her a box of condoms. Later that evening, as her daughter was preparing for a date, the mother told her about the situation and handed her a box of condoms. The girl burst out laughing and reached over to her mother, saying, "Oh Mom! You don't have to worry about that! I'm dating Susan!"

A couple took their 6-year-old son to the doctor. With some hesitation, they explained that although their little angel appeared to be in good health, they were concerned about his rather small penis.
After examining the child, the doctor confidently declared, "Just feed him pancakes. That should solve the problem."
The next morning when the boy arrived at breakfast, there was a large stack of warm

pancakes in the middle of the table." "Gee Mom!" he exclaimed. "Are these all for me?" The mother then replied, "Just take two, son. The rest are for your father."

A man and a woman are seated next to one another on a flight. They start eyeing each other and both realize they want to do the same thing. The man slips a condom out of his pocket, and she looks delighted. "Rear bathroom?" the man suggests. "Five minutes," replies the woman, and she goes off. The man waits five minutes, then goes to the bathroom and slips in with her. "Right, get that condom on," says the woman. Soon enough, they are sighing with pleasure.
Just then, a sharp-eyed stewardess notices them, and realizing what they are up to, humiliates the couple by making an announcement over the loudspeaker.
"To the lady and gentleman in the rear bathroom," she says. "We know what you are doing, and it is expressly forbidden by airline regulations. Now please, put out those cigarettes and take the condom off the smoke detector!"

Two policemen call the station on their radio.

"Hello... is this the Sarge?" they ask.

"Yes," he replies.

"We have a case here, Sarge," say the policemen. "A woman has shot her husband dead for stepping on the floor she has just mopped."

"Have you arrested the woman?" he asks.

"No sir," they say. "The floor is still wet."

JUDGE: Is your appearance today pursuant to a deposition I sent to your attorney?
MAN: No, this is how I dress when I go to work.

A country wife came home and saw her husband in bed with another woman. With strength borne of fury, cutting firewood and lifting sacks of feed, the woman dragged him down the stairs, across the yard and into the barn. She put his manhood in a vice, secured it tightly and removed the handle. Next, she picked up a carpenter's saw. The husband was horrified and screamed for her to stop, and asked in pure fear, "You're not going to cut it off with that rusty saw, are you?"

The wife, with a gleam of revenge in her eye, put the saw in her husband's hand and said, "Nope, you are! I'm going to burn down the barn!"

Two bees met in a field. One said to the other, "The weather has been cold, wet and damp and there aren't any flowers, so I can't make honey."

"No problem," replied the second bee. "Just fly down five blocks and turn left. Keep going until you see all the cars. There is a Bat Mitzvah going on, so there will be all sorts of fresh flowers and fresh fruit."

"Thanks for the tip," said the first bee, who flew away. A few hours later the two bees ran into each other again. The second bee asked, "How did it go?"

"Great!" said the first bee. "I found everything I wanted... plenty of fruit and floral arrangements on every table."

"But what's that thing on your head?" asked the second bee?

"My yarmulke," said the first bee. "I didn't want them to think I was a wasp."

Out at sea, there was a pirate ship sailing along. The ship's captain asked his shipmate in the crow's nest to keep lookout. All of a sudden, the man in the crow's nest noticed a ship approaching, and said that although the ship was a few miles off, it was gaining fast. The captain then said, "Quick! Someone get me my red shirt! This way, if I get hurt, the crew won't see and won't lose morale." The man on lookout then said, "They are getting closer, and now I see a fleet of five ships!" The captain then said, "Quick! Someone get me my brown pants!"

Three old men went into the pro-shop after having played 18 holes of golf. The pro asked about their game, and the first old guy said, "It was great... I had three riders today."
The second old guy said, "I had the most riders ever! I had five."
The last old man said, "I beat my old record. I had twelve riders today."
After they went into the locker room, another golfer who had overheard the old men went to the pro and said, "I've been playing golf for a long time and thought I

knew all the terminology, but what is a rider."

The pro said, "A rider is when you hit the ball far enough to actually get in the golf car and ride to it."

A man was walking through a seedy part of town and a bum asked him for two dollars. The man asked the bum if he would gamble it away or spend it on booze, and the bum said no. The man then asked the bum, "Will you come home with me so I can show my wife what happens to a man who doesn't drink or gamble?"

A shy man went into a bar and saw a beautiful woman sitting alone. After gathering up his courage for a half an hour, he finally asked her, "Would you mind if I chatted with you for a while?" The woman then yelled, at the top of her lungs, "No, I will not sleep with you tonight!" Everyone in the bar stared at the couple. Naturally, the shy man was hopelessly embarrassed and slunk back to his table. After a few moments, the woman went over to him and apologized. She smiled and said, "I'm sorry if I embarrassed you. You see, I am a journalist and I have an assignment to study how people respond to embarrassing situations."

The shy man responded, yelling at the top of his lungs, "What do you mean, two-hundred dollars?"

A merchant sent an urgent order to a distributer. Noticing the previous bill hadn't been paid, the collections officer notified the merchant that the order wouldn't be shipped until the bill was paid. The merchant then called back and said, "Cancel the order, we can't wait that long."

A photographer for a national magazine was assigned to get photos of a forest fire. The smoke at the scene was too thick to get any good shots, so he frantically called his home office to help him hire a plane. He was assured that the plane would be waiting for him at the airport. As soon as he got to the small, rural airport, sure enough a plane was warming up on the runway. The photographer jumped in with his equipment and yelled, "Let's go, let's go!" The pilot swung the plane into the wind and soon they were in the air.

"Fly over the north end of the fire," said the photographer, "and make three or four level passes."

"Why?" asked the pilot.

"Because I am going to take pictures!" exclaimed the photographer. "I am a photographer, and photographers take pictures!"

After a long pause, the pilot said, "Wait... you mean you're not the instructor?"

There was a nun who worked as a nurse at the local hospital. She was driving a hospital van one day when it ran out of gas about a mile from the gas station, so she decided to walk there to get some gas. However, the station didn't have a can for her to transport the gas back to her van. The nun then walked back to the van, trying to figure out what to do when she realized she had some bed pans she could use. So she got a bed pan and walked back to the station, filled it up, and brought it back to the van. As she was pouring the gas into the tank, two men in a truck drove by. Noticing the nun, one man said to the other, "Man, if that works I'm turning Catholic."

A worried woman paid a visit to her doctor. "I don't know what to do," she said. "My husband loses his temper for no reason, and it scares me." The doctor replied, "I have a cure. When your husband gets angry, take a gulp of water and swish it in your mouth. Don't swallow until he either leaves or gives up and goes to bed." Two weeks later, the woman returned happy as can be. She asked the doctor why such a simple remedy worked, and the doctor responded, "The water does nothing. It's keeping your mouth shut that does the trick."

This morning I lucked out and was able to buy several cases of ammunition. On the way home, I stopped by the gas station, where there was a drop dead gorgeous blonde filling her car up with gas. She looked over at my pile of ammo and said in a very alluring voice, "I'm a big believer in bartering, big boy. What do you say we trade some sex for some ammo." I thought it over and responded, "Well, just what kind of ammo do you have?"

An anatomy professor was giving a lecture on involuntary muscle contraction to his students. This was not an exciting subject, so the professor pointed to a woman in the front row and asked, "Do you know what your asshole is doing while you're having an orgasm?" She replied, "Probably out golfing with his buddies." It took 45 minutes to restore order in the classroom.

Two brothers enlisting in the army were getting their physicals. During the examination, the doctor was surprised to learn that both the men had incredibly long and oversized penises. "How do you account for this?" the doctor asked them.
"It's hereditary, sir," said the older brother.
"I see," said the doctor, writing this in his file. "Your father is responsible for your long penis?"
"No, sir," said the other brother. "Our mother is."
"Your mother?" said the doctor. "How is that possible? Women don't have penises.

"I know," replied the first brother. "But she only had one arm, and when it came to getting us out of the bathtub, she did the best she could."

MEDICAL ADVICE FROM A JEWISH SAGE

1. F***ing once a week is good for your health, but harmful if done every day.
2. F***ing relaxes your mind and body.
3. After f***ing, don't eat too much. Try to drink more liquids.
4. Try f***ing in bed, because it saves you energy.

So remember... FASTING is good for your health. May God cleanse your dirty mind.

A pastor's wife was expecting a baby, so he stood before the congregation and asked for a raise. After much discussion, they passed a rule that whenever the pastor's family expanded, so would his paycheck.
After six children, this started to get expensive, and the congregation decided to

hold another meeting to discuss the pastor's expanding salary.

A great deal of yelling and inner bickering ensued, and both sides of the decision were discussed.

After listening to them for about an hour, the pastor rose from his chair and spoke, "Children are a gift from God, and we will take as many gifts as He gives us." Silence fell over the congregation.

In the back pew, a little old lady struggled to stand, and finally in her frail voice she said, "Rain is also a gift from God, but when we get too much of it, we wear rubbers." The entire congregation said, "Amen."

Vinny and Sal are out in the woods hunting when suddenly Sal grabs his chest and falls to the ground. He doesn't seem to be breathing; his eyes are rolled back in his head. Vinny whips out his cell phone and calls 911. He tells the operator, "I think Sal is dead! What should I do?" The operator, in a calm, soothing voice says, "Just take it easy and follow my instructions. First, let's make sure he's dead."

There is a silence and then a gunshot is heard. Vinny's voice comes back on the line. "Okay . . . now what?"

While getting a checkup, a man tells his doctor that he thinks his wife is losing her hearing.
The doctor says, "You should do a simple test. Stand 15 feet behind her and say, 'Honey?' Move 3 feet closer and do it again. Keep moving 3 feet closer until she finally responds. Remember how close you were when she gives you an answer – it will help me know how bad her hearing loss is."
About a month later, the same guy is at the doctor again.
The doctor asks, "Well, did you do that experiment with your wife's hearing? Did it all work out?"
The man replied, "Yes."
"How close did you get before she answered?" asked the doctor.
The man replied, "Well, by the time I got about 3 feet away she just turned around and said, 'FOR THE FIFTH TIME . . . WHAT!?!?'"

A man and his wife went to the doctor.
The doctor took the husband in first.
The husband was a bit embarrassed and told the doctor he had trouble getting an erection with his wife and she was getting frustrated. The doctor checked his blood pressure and other things, then said he was going to check with the wife. The doctor took the wife to another cubicle and asked her to disrobe. Then he told her to turn all the way around slowly. She did as instructed.
He then told her to turn all the way around in the other direction.
Then he said, "Okay, good – you can get dressed now, and I will talk with your husband."
The doctor went back to the other cubicle and said to the husband, "Well, you can relax, there is nothing wrong with you. I couldn't get an erection either."

VINCENT VAN GOGH'S RELATIVES

His obnoxious brother: PLEASE GOGH

His nephew the psychoanalyst: E. GOGH

The ballroom dancer aunt: TAN GOGH

The constipated uncle: CAN'T GOGH

His dizzy aunt: VERTI GOGH

His prune-loving sister: GOTTA GOGH

His fruit-loving cousin: MAN GOGH

His convenience store owner cousin: STOP N GO

His prudish aunt: NO GOGH

His stubborn ex-wife: WON'T GOGH

And finally, his niece who travels the country in a huge R.V.: WINNIE BAY GOGH

THINGS YOU CAN SAY ONLY ON THANKSGIVING

Talk about a huge breast!

I'm in the mood for a little dark meat.

Are you ready for seconds yet?

Tying the legs together keeps the inside moist.

It's Cool Whip time!

If I don't undo my pants, I'll burst!

That's one terrific spread!

Just wait your turn – you'll get some.

Don't play with your meat.

Do you think you'll be able to handle all these people at once?

I didn't expect everyone to come at once.

You'll know it's ready when it pops up.

IN THE STOCKMARKET TODAY

Feathers were down and paper was stationery.
Weights were up in heavy trading.

Fluorescent tubes were down in light trading.

Light switches were off.

Caterpillar stock inched up a bit.

Knives were up sharply.

Cows were steered into a bull market.

Pencils were down a few points.

Hiking equipment was trailing.

Elevators went up, then down.

Escalators experienced slight decline.

Mining equipment hit rock bottom.

Diapers were unchanged.

Balloon prices were inflated.

Helium was up.

Sun peaked at mid-day.

Major shipping lines stayed on an even keel.

WOMAN STOPS GATOR ATTACK WITH A SMALL BERETTA PISTOL

While out walking along the edge of the bayou just below Houma, Louisiana, my soon-to-be ex-husband and I were discussing property settlement and other divorce issues. All of a sudden, we were surprised by a huge 12-foot alligator emerging from the murky water that started charging at us with its jaws wide open. This she-gator must have been protecting her nest because she was extremely aggressive. If I had not had my Beretta Jetfire .25 caliber pistol with me, I would not be here today. Just one shot to my estranged husband's kneecap was all it took! The gator got him easily and I was able to escape. It's one of the best pistols in my collection and what I saved in lawyer's fees was more than worth the purchase price of the gun!

A middle-aged woman had a heart-attack and was taken to the hospital. While on the operating table, she had a near-death experience. Seeing God, she said, "Is my time up?"

God said, "No. You have another 43 years, two months and eight days to live."

Since she had so much more time to live, she figured she might as well look even nicer. Upon recovery, the woman decided to stay in the hospital and have a face-lift, liposuction and a tummy-tuck.

After her last operation, she was released from the hospital. While crossing the street on her way home, an ambulance killed her. Arriving in heaven before God, the woman demanded, "I thought you said I had another 40 years! Why didn't you pull me out of the path of the ambulance?"

God replied, "Girl! I didn't recognize you!"

A very loud engineer from Texas was visiting Australia, and talking big about all the large civil works in the USA that he was involved in. To be polite, his Australian counterpart took him on a tour of some of Sydney's larger constructions. First he took him to the

Gladesville Bridge. The Texan exclaimed, "What's that?" and the Australian replied, "The Gladesville Bridge!"

"Hmmm," said the Texan. "How long and how many men did it take to build?"

The Australian replied, "About 5 years with 1,000 men."

The Texan replied, "Well, in Texas we would've done it in 2 years with 500 men."

Next, they went to the Sydney Opera House. "What's that?" asked the Texan and the Australian replied, "The Opera House."

"Hmmm," said the Texan. "How long and how many men did it take to build?"

The Australian replied, "About 10 years with 200 men."

The Texan replied, "Well, in Texas we would've done it in 4 years with 200 men."

By this stage, the Australian was a little put out by the Texan's attitude, so he decided to get back at him. They walked around the Opera House until the Sydney Harbor Bridge came into view.

The Texan exclaimed, "Wow! What's that?"

The Australian replied, "I don't know, it wasn't there yesterday."

In the back woods of Kentucky, a redneck's wife went into labor in the middle of the night and the doctor was called out to assist in the delivery. Since there was no electricity, the doctor handed the father-to-be a lantern and said, "Hold this high up so I can see what I am doing." Soon, a baby boy was born. "Whoa!" said the doctor. "Don't be in such a rush to put that lantern down! I think I see another baby coming!" Sure enough, within minutes he had delivered a baby girl. "Hold that lantern up! There's another coming!" exclaimed the doctor and sure enough, he delivered another baby girl. "Don't be in a hurry to put that lantern down," repeated the doctor. "It seems there is yet another one coming!"
The redneck scratched his head in bewilderment, and asked the doctor, "You reckon it might be the light that's attractin' 'em?"

Not too long ago, there was a woman who wanted to know how her husband would react if she left without telling him she was gone. She decided to write him a letter saying she was tired of him and didn't want to live with him anymore. After writing the letter, she put in on the table in the bedroom and climbed under the bed to hide until her husband was home. When he eventually got home, he saw the letter and read it. After a few moments of silence, he picked up a pen and added a few words to the letter. Then he began to whistle a happy tune and sing and dance. He grabbed his phone and dialed a number. The wife listened from under the bed as the husband began to speak.

"Hey babe," he said. "I'm just changing now and will join you soon. As for the other fool, it finally dawned on her that I was fooling around on the side, so she left. I was really wrong to have married her, and I wish you and I had met before I did. See you soon, honey!" He hung up and walked out of the room.

In tears and very upset, the wife climbed out from under the bed and stumbled over to read what her unfaithful husband had written. Through teary eyes, she read: "I could see your feet, you idiot! I am going out to buy bread."

Hospital regulations require a wheelchair for when a patient is discharged. However, while working as a student aide, John found one elderly gentleman already dressed and sitting on his bed with a suitcase packed at his feet, insisting that he needed no help to leave the hospital.

After a chat about the rules being rules for a reason, the man let John wheel him to the elevator. On the way down, John asked if his wife would be meeting him.

"I don't know," said the man. "She is still upstairs changing out of her hospital gown!"

Ever since I was a child, I have always feared someone hiding under my bed at night. So I went to see a psychiatrist. I told him I thought I was going crazy.

The psychiatrist replied, "I understand. Just put yourself in my care for three years, for three visits a week, and I will be able to take care of this fear."

"How much per visit?" I asked.

"100 dollars per session," he replied.

"I'll think on it." I replied.

Six months later, I saw the same

psychiatrist on the street. "Why didn't you come see me?" he asked.

"Well, 100 bucks three times a week for three years is a lot of money!" I said. "A bartender cured me for 10 dollars."

"Is that so?" said the psychiatrist. "And might I ask how the bartender cured you?"

"He told me to cut off the legs of the bed!" I said. "Ain't nobody there now!"

A man went to his lawyer and told him, "My neighbor owes me $500 and he won't pay up. What should I do?"

"Do you have any proof that he owes you the money?" asked the lawyer?

"Nope," replied the man.

"OK, then write him a letter asking for the $1,000 he owes you," said the lawyer.

"But it's only $500," said the man.

"Precisely," said the lawyer. "That's what he will reply, and then you'll have your proof!"

HILARIOUS ONE LINERS